ORNAMENTAL
GRASSES

An essential guide

CLIFF PLOWES

THE CROWOOD PRESS

First published in 2012 by
The Crowood Press Ltd
Ramsbury, Marlborough
Wiltshire SN8 2HR

www.crowood.com

British Library Cataloguing-in-Publication Data
A catalogue record for this book is available from the British Library.

ISBN 978 1 84797 382 5

Dedication
To my dear wife Gill, my partner in life and on the nursery, without whom none of this would have been possible or have any point.

Acknowledgements
Although I have written this book (and therefore all the errors are mine), it is really part of the story of Oak Tree Nursery, which owes its establishment and success as much, if not more, to my wife Gill as to me. The thanks to the following therefore come from us both.

All our parents, brothers and sisters who have helped in establishing the nursery, sometimes by just digging holes! Likewise, all our friends who also participated in the process; special mention should go to the Spilman family; Ruth couldn't stay around to see this book but would have loved the idea of it. Sadly, others too are no longer with us but are fondly remembered. All the staff at Askham Bryan College, York. who managed to instil some horticultural knowledge into me. Roger Brooks, Alan Thompson and Dr Bruce Rigby were notable influences. My fellow exhibitors at all the flower shows who have always been generous with their time, expertise and friendship. Special to us are Val and Bob Smith, who have eased the workload for me at many a show, and, of course, the Silver Fox. All those at the RHS Shows Department who had faith in what we were doing, particularly all the Show Managers both past and present. Our staff (who are really our friends): Angela, Kate and Christine. We couldn't have produced the plants without you all. The biggest thank you goes to Neil Lucas of Knoll Gardens who has guided and inspired me and shown me the true beauty and value of ornamental grasses.

Image Acknowledgements
I am truly indebted to Neil Lucas for the images of Knoll gardens; Lady Caroline Legard for allowing such generous access to the Walled Garden at Scampston in North Yorkshire; and to all others who have kindly allowed me to photograph their grasses. All images are by Cliff Plowes unless credited in the caption.

Typeset by Jean Cussons Typesetting, Diss, Norfolk
Printed and bound in China by Everbest Printing Co Ltd

ORNAMENTAL
GRASSES

An essential guide

Contents

Foreword

When garden designer Gertrude Jekyll made the planting of the Great Plat at *Hestercombe* Garden in Somerset, UK, she used clumps of *Miscanthus* as a key component of the design. Jekyll recognized the value of grasses as important structural plants, creating a sense of cohesion in the design. She appreciated their movement, form, structure and colour, all provided over a longer period than just about any other 'herbaceous' perennial. That it was over 100 years ago that Jekyll designed the planting of the Great Plat says two things; that she was far-sighted in her plant selection for the project, and that it has taken grasses a long, long time to truly seep into the gardening public's consciousness, for these are plants that are still considered 'new' by a surprisingly large number of gardeners.

But the moment one sees grasses used well, whether as a component of a mixed planting with flowering perennials or shrubs, planted in great single-species swathes, or included alongside 'old-fashioned' plants such as roses, one instantly understands just how invaluable they are, and that all the qualities Jekyll appreciated make them superb choices for the garden.

What Jekyll wouldn't have known about, though, is the tremendous range of grasses available to gardeners today, with something for just about every possible situation. Visitors to flower shows that take place across the UK will often get an introduction to this amazing diversity from a visit to Cliff Plowes' Oak Tree Nursery stand. The plants he presents at those shows demonstrate the extraordinary range of conditions that grasses and grass-like plants can tolerate, as well as the variety of size, form and colour available, all of them displayed to perfection with the expert eye of a really knowledgeable grower.

Cliff's long knowledge is distilled in this book, and the expertise he has accrued in showing plants to the highest standard, and the intimate knowledge of the plants at hand, can also be invaluable to the home gardener in getting the most out of their plants and really enjoying their potential. Grasses are great, not just because of their superb qualities and huge variety, but also for their suitability for gardens of all sizes and locations. Not only are they beautiful to look at, but they are also a most democratic group of plants, available to all, tough, usually pest- and disease-free and mostly easy to grow. I wouldn't be without them.

Matthew Wilson, garden designer, writer, broadcaster and MD of Clifton Nurseries in London

OPPOSITE: *Panicum* with Viburnum 'Lanarth'.

Introduction

Garden designs, and therefore the plants used, are shaped by trends and new ideas of what is current. We may therefore think that, given the increasingly widespread use of ornamental grasses as decorative plants, this is a new phenomenon. However, it is not the case because we can trace ornamental grasses back to the plant lists of nurseries in England around 1600. The great difference is that today we have a far greater choice of varieties to utilize and you are likely to see grasses used in all types of planting schemes, from domestic gardens through amenity planting to botanical gardens. The testimony that grasses have ornamental value is illustrated by their inclusion in the plant catalogue of John Parkinson in 1640, at a time when plants were used either as medicinal herbs, objects of interest and curiosity, or a statement of personal wealth by the landed gentry. Although the varieties used were mostly grasses native to England and her nearby trading partners, nevertheless the beauty and interesting form of grasses were established.

The next big leap forward in the use of grasses came with the fashion of botanizing, the collecting and planting of all the subjects of a particular order of plant. In 1740 Humphrey Repton designed such a garden for Woburn Abbey, using only grasses. By now the range of species was growing due to the many trade links built up by merchants and plant hunters. Foremost amongst collectors, although not now commonly known, was John Bartram, an American who sent regular collections of seeds and plants to the eager gardeners of Britain.

William Robinson lists some thirty ornamental grasses in his *The English Flower Garden* (1883). Robinson was passionate in championing the idea of what he termed 'naturalization'. In his previous book, *The Wild Garden* (1870), he gives a list of British native grasses that could be used in a wild garden. The English garden designer Gertrude Jekyll pioneered the use of grasses in the herbaceous border, and using the tall species as focal points and others as woodland carpeting plants. One of her favourite foliage grasses was *Leymus arenarius*, which she realized had the perfect colour to fit in with other blue and grey herbaceous plants.

The availability of a wider range of grasses and their use in their own right only began in earnest in the 1950s. A German garden designer and nurseryman, Karl Foerster, pioneered the use of grasses to provide an all-season approach to the garden rather than the previous thinking of 'down' times in the garden. He realized the potential for grasses to provide interest in the autumn and winter and wrote several books on plant associations and the use of grasses in the garden. Foerster's ideas found favour with like-minded garden designers Roberto Burle Marx and Wolfgang Oehme, who took his ideas to America. Richard Simon worked

---

Pioneer dates of ornamental grasses

Decorative grasses used in the seventeenth century (1640):

- Great Quaking Grass (*Briza maxima*)
- Cotton Grass (*Eriophroram angustifolium*)
- Pearl Barley (*Hordeum vulgare* var. *bexastichum*)
- Job's Tears (*Coix lacryma-jobi*)
- Ribbon Grass (*Phalaris arundinacea*)
- Feather Grass (*Stipa pennata*)
- First listing as an ornamental plant in 1782 in the catalogue of John Kingston Galpine.
- Next mentioned in 1883: thirty listed as ornamentals by William Robinson.

OPPOSITE: *Miscanthus nepalensis* and *Gaura lindheimerii*.

Coix lacryma-jobi (Job's tears).
Common in herb gardens in
the fourteenth century, its
fruit was known to be used
medicinally in 1596 in India.
The dried seed heads were
used in rosaries.

in Switzerland after graduating from Cornell University and here he met Kurt Bluemel. Some years later, they worked together at Bluemount, Simon's family nursery. The collaboration of Bluemel and Simon with Oehme made Bluemount Nurseries the first American nursery to grow and sell a range of ornamental grasses. Some years later Kurt Bluemel started his own renowned nursery supplying grasses to the landscape trade.

Back in Germany, Ernst Pagels was producing a whole new range of Miscanthus by crossing *Miscanthus sinensis* 'Gracillimus' with other varieties. These stunning new varieties helped further the interest in grasses as worthy garden plants. In England the work done by Blooms of Bressingham in introducing grasses into their gardens and using them with other plants did much to gain a foothold for ornamental grasses as garden plants of merit. Beth Chatto's gardens also showed how grasses could be used in difficult areas such as dry gardens.

Today we benefit from all the previous work carried out in selecting and developing the wide range of grasses at our disposal. There are grasses to suit every location and condition and their appeal and usefulness have been realized and developed by the landscape designers. However, grasses could still be used more in our domestic gardens. The aim of this book is both to expand the knowledge of those gardeners who have already begun to use some grasses in their gardens, and to encourage and demystify the subject for those thinking of introducing grasses to their gardens.

It is not the intention of this book to discuss in depth the use of grasses in garden design, a subject worthy of a book of its own; a selection of these can be found in the appendix. The content of this book is based on the questions most frequently asked by gardeners at the many flower shows I attend, coupled with the knowledge I have built up, and gained from other growers of grasses, over the fifteen years that my wife and I have been growing ornamental grasses in our nursery.

Leymus arenarius (Lyme grass). The glaucous blue foliage was a favourite with Gertrude Jekyll.

1 What is an ornamental grass?

The term 'ornamental grasses' is used by gardeners and landscape designers to describe a plant that looks 'grass-like'. That is, it usually forms a clump-like structure, is often made up of fine leaves, and does not have a large decorative flower made up of petals. This is an accepted and useful description when dealing with the group of plants but is in fact far short of the mark botanically. What might seem a very simple plant form is actually a group of different plants that have evolved along similar lines. Understanding their botanical characteristics and the way they have developed will help in the cultivation of the plant in a garden situation, and is an interesting study that should add to the gardener's appreciation and enjoyment.

The plants known as ornamental grasses are a small selection of plants from different plant families that are sufficiently grass-like in their appearances to be included in grass planting schemes or collections; they are usually made up of six groups of plants:

- True grasses (Poaceae)
- Sedges (Cyperaceae)
- Rushes (Juncaceae)
- Cat-Tails (Typhaceae)
- Restios (Restionaneae)
- Grass-like plants

The majority of these groups belong to a group of plants known as monocotyledons, plants having one seed leaf ('mono' means one and 'cotyledon' is the seed leaf). The veins of monocotyledons run parallel to each other along the length of the leaf. Most have smooth edges as opposed to being toothed or notched. Nearly all the group are herbaceous, that is, they do not form woody tissue with age, the exception being bamboos (the Poaceae family), which form canes.

TRUE GRASSES

The true grasses belong to the family Poaceae; they can also be referred to as being in the family Graminaceae, an older name for the same family, but Poaceae is the preferred modern usage. The grasses are the most important family of plants for the existence and development of the human species. Whether in the form of direct fodder or animal feed, they provide food for all grazing animals raised to provide meat for our consumption. All the cereal grains are members of the grass family, providing flour and also the rice that is the basis for existence of a major part of the earth's population.

Pennisetum villosum (Feather grass). A true grass that originates from the mountains of tropical Africa. It tolerates a little frost, and should be treated as an annual in cold, wet climates.

OPPOSITE: Late summer foliage colour and seed heads add interest to the Panicum family of grasses.

Characteristics of true grasses

The leaf of grasses is flat and arranged in two rows growing alternately along the sides of the stem. The stem in grasses is known as the culm and is, in most cases, hollow. It is split into sections by joints called nodes, which are solid and to which the leaf is attached. On most plants, the growing point is at the tip of the leaf or shoot; this is not so in grasses and has given them an advantage in their survival. Grasses have two growing points, one at the base and one at the node. This means that if the tip of the plant is grazed off or removed, it can grow again from the point at the node; or, in a situation where it has been cut down to the ground, from the growing point deep in the base of the plant.

Because grasses have developed to be wind-pollinated, they have no need to attract insects by producing large or showy petalled flowers. Grasses do, of course, produce flowers but in most cases these are small and green. The flower clusters of grasses are called inflorescences. These are often referred to by gardeners as seed heads, due to the fact that they do not produce the bright petals that are commonly recognized as flower heads. Inflorescences fall into three types: spikes, racemes and panicles. It is the inflorescences that give the added beauty to grasses, as they change in form and colour from first emerging to the time they have produced their seed.

SEDGES

Sedges belong to the family Cyperaceae. Smaller in number than the grasses, they are still a relatively large family. Unlike the grass family, they are of limited commercial value to humans and are not a food sources for animals. Their greatest contribution is in the production of papyrus paper and the raw material for some basketwork and mat weaving.

Characteristics of sedges

In section the leaves of sedges are usually v-shaped, and their stems are triangular. This is a good identification aid because if the stem is held between finger and thumb and rotated gently, the different sides can clearly be felt. Unlike grasses, the stems of sedge are solid and have no nodes. Sedges usually don't develop the large showy inflorescences of the grass family. An interesting feature, particularly in the Carex genus, is that the plant will carry both male and female flower spikes, usually one above the other. The white stigmas of the female plant contrast with the dark brown male spike on *Carex elata* 'Aurea' and provide an attractive feature. Other Carex can have an inflated spiky sac containing the female flower; this is called a utricle and is green in colour. It is retained until the seeds develop and ripen, gradually turning brown as it dries out. *Carex lupulina* and *Carex Grayi* both have this feature.

RUSHES

These belong to the Juncaceae family. They are less grass-like in appearance than true grasses and sedges and of no major economic importance. Two genus of the group *Juncus* (the true rushes) and *Luzula* (wood rushes) provide attractive, and in some cases unusual, garden subjects.

Carex pendula (Pendulous sedge). A typical sedge that originated in West and Central Europe and North Africa.

Characteristics of rushes

Two forms of leaf are present. In the wood rushes, the leaf is flat and the growth of the plant basal and usually quite low. Small white hairs can be detected on the edge and underside of the leaf. The true rushes usually have an upright habit and the leaf is thin, cylindrical in section and solid.

The inflorescences are more like a conventional flower in appearance but very small, usually white in colour. On the true rushes, they appear about two thirds of the way up the stem. In the wood rushes, they are borne on stems above the basal clump of the plant at differing heights depending on the species.

CAT-TAILS

The cat-tail family is the smallest of the grass-like group and perhaps the most ungrasslike in its appearance. It comprises one genus, *Typha*, and is therefore in the Typhaceae family.

Characteristics of cat-tails

Although a small family, cat-tails are invariably present in any wetland planting scheme. They need water or

Typha latifolia (common cat-tail). A typical cat-tail flowerhead. This is a mature female spike.

bog-like conditions to flourish. The leaves are strap-like and erect, borne in pairs from the base. The inflorescence is the main feature of the plant: borne on a single stem, it resembles a cigar in appearance, comprised of many tightly-packed female flowers with a single fluffy male flower on the top. Beginning green, the female flowers eventually turn brown and then slowly disintegrate through the season. It is commonly called a reed mace but frequently, and erroneously, a bulrush.

RESTIOS

Belonging to the family Restionaceae, these are rushlike in appearance but do not share the same cultural requirements. They are the most recently introduced

Juncus patens 'Carmen's Grey' (California grey rush). A typical rush – stiff, erect, with cylindrical stems. This variety was introduced by Carmen's Nursery, California.

Chondropetalum tectorum. A typical restio, originating from the South African Cape region.

Lilyturf. The Acorus genus, which includes a number of excellent coloured specimens, is often included in this group although it has no grass reference in its name. The smaller irises and sisyrinchiums could be taken for grasses until the flowers are produced. Libertias also fit into this group, having strappy leaves; *Libertia peregrinans* is sometimes referred to as golden reed.

None of this group produces the graceful inflorescences of grasses but they often contribute a block of evergreen colour to a planting scheme and resemble grasses closely enough to fit in happily with them. What fits into the group is, in some cases, a matter of personal choice but in general the required characteristic is that the foliage is the main feature of the plant.

and least seen of the grass-like family, mainly due to the specialized treatment the seed requires to germinate. Being from a warm climate, only a small number will be winter hardy in cold-temperature climates.

Characteristics of restios

Mostly rushlike in appearance, restios rarely develop a leaf system but do have a leaf sheath at the node that is attractively coloured gold or tan brown. The stems are cylindrical and either solid or hollow; flower heads are in green or brown spikelets.

GRASS-LIKE PLANTS

The plants that fit into this group are not botanically grasses. However, because of their similarity in appearance to grasses, they are used in grass planting schemes or to complement a collection of grasses.

In some cases, the common name of the plant reflects its grass-like appearance. *Ophiopogon intermedius* is known as Mondo Grass; *Ophiopogon planiscapus* 'Nigrescens' is commonly known as Black Grass or Black Mondo; *Liriope muscari* is known as

Ornamental grasses?

Having made the distinction between the families that make up ornamental grasses, for the rest of the book I will refer to them as grasses. It is very useful to know the family a plant belongs to as a guide to giving it the right conditions for successful growth. However, because the grass family has colonized most of the globe, various members have adapted to grow in conditions in which the majority of the family would not thrive. For example, most of the sedge family prefer damp soils, but some prefer a free-draining soil. And because grasses have grown all over the world, the conditions they are used to in their natural habitat may not be replicated in the country where a gardener wishes to grow them. A natural occurrence of high rainfall may suit a plant in its native environment, but it may not be used to low temperatures. The combination of wet and cold in a different part of the world could be too much for the plant to tolerate. The answer is to grow it in a more free-draining soil in its non-native country. Therefore, it is always best to use the specific recommendations for individual species within a group, rather than what could be considered the family norm.

The family of ornamental grasses

'Sedges have edges and rushes are round but grasses have nodes from their tips to the ground.'

True grasses (Poaceae): 600 genera and 9,000 species. Grow on every continent and occur natively from the Arctic to Antarctica.

Sedges (Cyperaceae): 115 genera and 3,600 species. Grow in most parts of the world, particularly in wet areas.

Rushes (Juncaceae): ten genera, 400 species. Grow in most parts of the world.

Restios (Restionaceae): thirty-eight genera, 400 species. Grow almost exclusively in the southern hemisphere.

Cat-tails (Typhaceae): one genus and fifteen species. Grows in freshwater habitats throughout the world.

Liriope muscari 'John Burch' (turf lily). Obviously not a grass, but when not in flower, its grass-like foliage allows the plant to be used in grass schemes.

2 The growing habits of grasses

When considering using grasses in a garden situation, there are a few points to bear in mind.

Firstly, is a permanent planting scheme needed or will a one-year scheme suffice for the area? If the answer is permanent, then perennial grasses would be most suitable. A one-year scheme can be easily achieved by the use of annual grasses.

Secondly, if the scheme is permanent, would foliage be required year round? This may be the case if you are using plants to screen an area or an object, or to provide a background to other plants. If that is so, then evergreen grasses would be the ideal choice.

Thirdly, consider the space available for the grass to grow in. Grasses have two forms of spreading growth: they are runners or clump formers. The runners spread by the use of rhizomes or stolons, which move away from the mother plant to form new plants and can 'move' considerable distances. Clumps expand by sending up new growth at the outside limit of the plant, thus making a tight clump.

RUNNERS OR CLUMPERS

The characteristic growth method of a particular grass should not be regarded as a negative point. Rather, with a little consideration of what is required of the grass, it can be a positive advantage.

Runners

Grasses with a running habit can be used to great effect when you need to cover large areas quickly. Because of their running habit, many will quickly form a dense carpet, providing good ground cover in a short time. The rhizomes also have the ability to bind together loose soils. This can be a great advantage when planting

Phalaris arundinacea 'Feesey' (Reed canary grass). Spreading by runners, Phalaris can overwhelm a smaller garden so should be used with care.

OPPOSITE: *Miscanthus*, *Eupatorium*, *Echinacea* and *Verbena* in the Decennium border at Knoll Gardens.

Useful terms

Annual grasses: plants that complete their entire life cycle from seed to reproduction to death in one year.

Perennial grasses: plants that grow and reproduce for many years; evergreen grasses having living leaves throughout the year.

Deciduous grasses: plants that shed their leaves at least once a year and remain leafless for weeks or months. Some grasses will retain the dead foliage throughout the winter.

Rhizome: a stem that grows along under the ground, bearing buds that grow into new plants.

Stolon: a stem that grows along the ground producing new plants at its nodes.

up difficult areas like slopes and banking. However, consideration would have to be given to the adjacent plantings because the runners will just keep going. This can be a disadvantage if the adjacent planting consists of slower growing species, in, say, a herbaceous border that would not be able to withstand intrusion by the grass. Large shrub plantings or trees, however, could easily cope. Cultural control can be used by selectively taking out the encroaching runners but this has to be done on a regular basis.

The climate and cultural conditions will have a bearing on the growth rate of the grass. For instance, a grass that originates from an area with a long warm season will be considerably slowed if planted in a climate with a shorter warm season, such as that of the UK.

Clumpers

The clump-forming grasses, by contrast, are far more predictable in their ultimate growth size. Additionally, they may take much longer to reach their ultimate size, due to the slower rate of reproduction. These two factors make them preferable for small gardens and garden designs requiring a more formal look, because they all create a particular shape that just increases in size every season. The disadvantage of this is that space has to be left for the plants to grow

The growth habit of grasses

Clumping grasses: form a tight mound and spread outwards by adding new growth to this mound every year. The speed at which they do this varies but is usually at a steady rate. They will keep the same shape but will just get wider.

Running grasses: spread by sending out rhizomes or stolons. New plants grow at points along their length. By this means they can cover large areas of ground as each new plant then matures to full size. The plant will continue to colonize surrounding areas and will not stop unless grown in a container or a raised bed.

Seeders: some grasses come true from seed. The mature grass produces viable seed that spreads by wind or animal distribution to different parts of the garden. If it finds a suitable site, it will germinate and produce new plants from this seed the following year. This is true of most annual grasses, with the difference that the original grass that produced the seed will die at the end of the year.

to their ultimate size. This usually means that extra maintenance has to be carried out on those areas to keep them weed free.

Festuca glauca. This specimen shows the neat clumping habit that makes this species ideal for small gardens in a sunny site.

COOL OR WARM SEASON GROWERS

Because most ornamental grasses have developed in either temperate or Mediterranean regions of the world, their growth cycles have developed to suit these conditions. A basic understanding of the two different growth patterns will assist in the selection of grasses to suit particular areas and temperature ranges.

Cool season growing grasses

As suggested by their name, cool season growers start into growth in the late winter. They develop reasonable amounts of foliage by early spring and can flower any time from late winter to early summer. The increase in temperature and decrease in rainfall during the summer months do not provide the optimum growing conditions for the cool season growers, so they go either into part or full dormancy. The best time to lift and divide them is from late winter to early spring.

Cool season grasses

Achnatherum
Agrostis canina
Arundinacea gigantea ssp. Tecta
Briza
Carex
Deschampsia
Festuca
Hakonechloa macra
Koeleria glauca
Melica
Milium effusum
Phalaris arundinacea
Stipa
Uncinia

Warm season growing grasses

Warm season growers are better developed to deal with the conditions encountered in summer. They start regrowth in late spring and grow very steadily until early summer when they reach full growing potential. Flowering takes place in late summer. With the onset of the cooler temperatures, they shut down and remain dormant through the winter. Lifting and division is best undertaken in late spring or early summer: certainly when the grass is making growth, but well away from its flowering period.

Warm season grasses

Andropogon gerardii
Arundo donax
Chasmanthium latifolium
Cortaderia
Elymus
Miscanthus
Molinia
Panicum virgatum
Pennisetum
Saccharum ravennae
Sorghastum nutans
Spartina pectinata 'Aureomarginata'

ANNUAL GRASSES

The majority of the grass family have developed along the perennial route to colonize and thrive. However, there are a small number of grasses that are annuals. The fact that they have just one year to germinate, grow and produce seed for the continuation of their species has resulted in some amazing seed heads and a high percentage of germination from the seeds produced.

To some degree this has also been the reason why they are not more popular as garden plants. If used in the wrong situation or not managed, they will colonize the garden with a determination born of survival. This attribute should not be looked upon as a negative factor; with a little careful planning and control of the resulting plants, annual grasses can bring an extra dimension of interest to a garden.

Where to use annual grasses

There are a number of situations where the annual grass's characteristic quick and successful germination can be an asset. They can produce a large number of plants that can be used to fill in a newly-planted scheme of herbaceous plants or perennial grasses until the intended planting has reached maturity. In containers, their interesting seed heads can be fully appreciated and provide a welcome change from the usual bedding annuals. If chosen carefully, they could be left to colonize an area of ground that may not be used as part of the formal garden or may be difficult to cultivate, such as a sunny bank. Mixed in with a selection of annual flowering plants, they can provide a prairie feel to an area.

Another use for annual grasses is as dried flowers because all their seed heads are showy and interesting. If this is the intended use, the seed heads should be picked before they have reached maturity and then dried in a light, dry place with good air circulation. If they are left to mature on the plant, they will quickly fall once they are ripe as this is how the species are so successful at reproducing.

If there is concern that the annual grasses could 'take over' the garden, it is best to remove the seed heads before they become mature and self-seed. However, this in some way defeats the object of using the grass in the first place. A halfway measure would be to remove a percentage of the seed heads as they become mature and leave a small number to continue the show.

The remaining seed can then be dried and sown the following spring for a second crop as most species come true from seed. If they are grown under glass to make plants in the second year, any self-germinated seedlings can be hoed off before they become a problem.

How to raise annual grasses

There are two options for growing annual grasses: firstly, sown directly *in situ* into the ground; secondly, as plants formed by raising seedlings in a greenhouse and clumping them together to form one plant. Which approach is taken depends on the ultimate use of the grass. If specimens are required for planting up in pots or as feature plants in a border, then the second option is preferable. If they are to be used as fillers amongst other plants, then the first option can be used.

As all annuals have to complete their life cycle in one year, it requires a reasonably long summer to achieve this. In areas with a short summer period, or if working to a specific deadline, the best option is to sow under glass early in the season and plant out when a reasonable size.

Sowing direct into the ground

Most annuals prefer a sunny site and a free-draining soil, so this is the first requisite of the outdoor site. A fine tilth should be achieved by raking over the ground and removing any stones and debris. An important factor to bear in mind is that the ground may already contain a number of wildflower seeds (in the garden situation, known as weeds) and the raking will bring these nearer to the surface ready to germinate at the same time as your annual grass seeds. This will result in a crop of young seedlings that make the grasses indistinguishable. The more vigorous weeds will outstrip the grasses in growth and smother them. This can be avoided by sowing the grass seed into wide drills (14in or 36cm). These drills can be spaced a width apart and marked by plant labels. Thus you can be sure that any seedlings outside these drills are unwanted and remove them at an early stage, and that your grass seedlings will be in the majority within the drills. Germination will usually take between fourteen and twenty-one days. When sowing allow roughly 1in between seeds and cover with light soil or sand. If you feel you have sown too thickly, thin out the seedlings when they are about 3in tall, removing the weakest.

Sowing annuals under glass

If a small number of single plants are required to spot plant through a border, to use in pots, or as part of a bedding scheme, then sowing under glass is recommended, using either a cold glasshouse or garden frame. Sow in early spring when the air temperature is warming up. Two sowing techniques could be used.

The first is to sow seeds directly into a 3in (8cm) pot, covering them with a thin layer of sand or vermiculite. Keep just moist and place in a cold greenhouse or cold frame. The seedlings should germinate in about fourteen days, producing a lawn-like appearance on the pot. Do not sow too thickly as the seedlings could crowd each other out, producing weak plants. When the seedlings reach about 2in (5cm) in height, prick small clumps out (about three or five seedlings in a bunch) into individual pots (7cm size). This group of seedlings will grow into each other and form one plant that can then be planted out later in the season.

The second method is to sow the seeds into modular trays, about three seeds per module, and let them grow on together. This removes the pricking out stage of the first method and avoids root disturbance. The seedlings will grow into each other and can then be potted on into a small pot to continue growing until big enough to plant out.

Because of the short life span and differing uses of annual grasses, it seems sensible to give a brief description of the characteristics of the most commonly used ones here rather than in the chapter on perennial grasses. As mentioned previously, some need a long warm growing season and so will be more successful in countries with a longer and warmer spring and summer than in the UK. If you are planning a bedding scheme using annual grasses as a main feature, you should bear this in mind and select suitable species

Briza maxima, showing the large seed heads that make an excellent dried subject.

from the many varieties that are available. The seed merchants are constantly bringing out new varieties of annual grasses with differing heads and seed colours so the following list should not be taken as definitive. The omission of any particular variety or species does not imply that it is not suitable or attractive to grow, only that local conditions and performance should be a main consideration.

Aira elegantissima (Hair Grass)
Low-growing grass, 10in (25cm), dense in appearance with very fine branches tipped by a minute spikelet. Resembles a silver cloud positioned above the plant.

Avena sterilis (Animated Oat)
Medium height grass, 3ft (90cm), so named because the long awls it produces twist as the humidity changes.

Briza maxima (Larger Quaking Grass)
Perhaps the best-known annual grass. *Maxima* produces the biggest spikelets of the *Briza* family, locket shaped and made up of overlapping scales. It grows to about 12in (30cm). Naturalized in England in about 1633 and known by different names in different parts of the country, but familiar to people who played in meadows as children and picked the grass when dry and rattled the seed heads.

Setaria 'Red Jewel' – a stunning annual grass that can be used in herbaceous borders to give height and interest.

Hordeum jubatum (Squirrel Tail Grass, Foxtail Barley)
Growing to 18in (45cm), the plant produces barley-like heads that are tinted pink.

Lagurus ovatus (Hare's Tail Grass)
Producing flame-shaped tails, it grows to 18in (45cm). The smaller version, *Lagurus ovatus* subsp. *nanus* grows to 6in (15cm) and is known as 'Bunny Tails'.

Lamarckia aurea (Goldentop Grass, Golden Dog's Tail)
Spike-like inflorescence with awns that point backwards, silky and yellow in appearance. Height 15in (40cm).

Panicum miliaceum (Purple Hog Millet)
The variety 'Violaceum' has panicles of green colour turning to deep purple throughout the season. Height 3ft (90cm).

Setaria macrostachys (Foxtail Millet)
Tall at 3ft (90cm), broad leaved with a fluffy head and droops with age. A number of cultivars are available with different coloured heads.

Stenotaphrum secundatum 'Variegatum' (St Augustine's Grass)
Evergreen, spreading by rhizomes. Leaves mid-green with cream stripe. Frost tender, but in warm climates is used as a coarse-textured lawn grass. Useful for containers and hanging baskets.

Zea mays (Indian Corn)
A family of very tall, broad leaved grasses, some reaching 8ft (2.4m) in the UK and even taller in warmer climes. Grown either for their colourful striped leaves or multicoloured cobs.

Bromus madritensis (Compact Brome)
Growing to about 2ft (60cm), the plant forms bunches of coarse, bristled spikes. It can be grown in shade.

Catapodium rigidum (Fern Grass)
A small plant, 9in (20cm), producing panicles that resemble fern fronds. The whole plant becomes rigid, starts green and turns to a bronze colour through the season.

Coix lacryma-jobi (Job's Tears)
A plant that needs a long, warm growing season. It grows to 12–18in (30–45cm) and produces large colourful seeds that were once used to make necklaces and rosaries.

OPPOSITE: *Stenotaphrum secundatum* 'Variegatum' (St Augustine grass). Evergreen, spreading by rhizomes. Its leaves are mid green with cream stripes. It is frost tender and useful for containers and hanging baskets.

3 Grasses grown in containers

The practice of growing plants in some kind of container has grown steadily over the past few years. This is partly due to the number of properties built without gardens of any size, or where the garden space is utilized as a play area for children by growing families with a limited amount of time to spend maintaining a garden. Growing a number of plants in containers therefore meets the requirement, and hopefully the desire, to have plants growing in the garden.

Containers have also found a home on outside eating areas and patios, which have also grown in popularity over the last few years. Here they can act as a link between the garden proper and the house, and bring a softness and interest element to what may otherwise be quite a utilitarian area.

To some extent, this trend has been helped by two factors. Firstly, garden designers and horticultural journalists have demonstrated the effects that can be achieved with a little planning and careful selection of containers and plant. Gone are the days when any plant was put into any plastic pot and stood in isolation in the garden without thought as to its purpose or requirements.

Secondly, the range of materials and shapes now available is huge, compared with, say, twenty years ago.

CONTAINERS

The word container covers a wide range of options, from a single, reasonably-sized pot, perhaps the size of a domestic bucket, to the beds that can be seen on roof gardens or the raised beds around courtyards. These are in essence still containers and to some degree require the same considerations as planning and planting up a single pot. The main consideration is 'Can the container provide a good growing environment for a plant?' To do this, two of the basic requirements are the plant's need for moisture and enough space to expand its roots. A further consideration is the position of the container with regard to sun and shade and extremes of weather, wind for instance. If these requirements are met by existing containers, or are borne in mind when purchasing new containers, the displays and effects that can be achieved can be stunning.

Choosing a container

The first thing to decide is what size of container is required. If the area where the container is to be sited is not large, or is a narrow thoroughfare, then a large container is not going to work. Conversely, one small container in a large area does not create enough impact, although here there is the option to use a number of containers of differing heights and widths grouped together to create the most interesting possibilities, rather than going for one single planter.

Having determined the size, you then need to decide on the shape. Is a tall planter needed, perhaps to stand at the side of a door or between two windows? Or is something lower required to fill a corner or stand on an area that has views beyond that are interesting and shouldn't be obscured?

You may have noted that so far what is to be grown in this container has not been mentioned.

RIGHT: A selection of terracotta pots showing the variety of shape and size available, from traditional finish to glazed..

OPPOSITE: This pair of modern pots are planted with *Pennisetum* 'Frosted Explosion'.

There is a strong case for using grasses in containers, and in most cases a grass can be found to meet all the required criteria. It is important, however, that any plant is chosen to fit the constraints and position of the container, not the other way round.

Materials

Traditionally, the options for containers were either terracotta or stone. Because of the integrity of these materials, they are still an excellent choice. However, the weight of both materials may rule them out, either because of their position (for example, on a roof garden), or for ease of movement.

Initially, when plastic containers were introduced, the colour (usually white!) and standard of construction were poor. Unfortunately, these negative points have left a legacy that tends to influence people's initial choice of materials. Today's plastic containers are far

superior and it is now acceptable to choose plastic as a material in its own right, rather than pretending to be a different material.

Technology has enabled the production of large, strong containers to be produced in fibreglass and other composite materials that do not have the weight problems of stone and are acceptable substitutes for more traditional materials such as lead planters or glazed pots. Again, as in the case of plastic, composite materials are quite acceptable in their own right and often suit modern development.

Steel is also now in common use as a material. It is always used in its own right and never masquerades as other materials. Perhaps it is best used in its clean silver form in a sympathetic combination with new architecture. However, there are some very acceptable rusted metal containers, and with the correct planting the colour and texture of the metal makes an attractive combination.

Wood is obviously a traditional material that has been in use for many years, usually to produce planters of a carpentry standard, and these can still have a place in the correct setting. Of late, however, timber has been used in a more unfinished state to produce large beds, and the various grains and textures of woods are used and developed for their own beauty.

Objects that had a former life can also be pressed into use as containers. The range of these is vast and if the scheme is carried out with care and a thoughtful use of plant material, it can be very successful and attractive. If not, it looks a complete disaster.

Requirements of a container

Whatever materials, colour or style you decide on, to be a success every container needs to be able to provide the following basic requirements for a plant's well-being.

Water

All plants need water to grow successfully, some more than others depending on their growing habit. It is essential, therefore, that the containers are easy to water once they are planted up and that enough water can be provided to sustain growth. For larger plants, it may be necessary to install some form of automatic watering system. This should also be a serious consideration if the plants are to be left for long periods without attention. Providing a container

The traditional material of wood, used here to construct a stylish looking planter. Planted with *Calamagrostis* 'Overdam'.

with enough water basically means leaving an adequate space between the planter rim, and the compost so that the necessary amount of water can be added and allowed to soak into the rooting area of the plants. Also take into consideration that some materials such as terracotta are porous and that moisture will be lost through evaporation. Other materials such as metals will retain and conduct heat very efficiently and so the compost will dry out more quickly.

Conversely, most plants do not like being in waterlogged conditions, so adequate drainage has to be provided. In its simplest form, this is provided by drainage holes in the base of the container. Care should be taken that they are large enough and spaced out over the base of the pot to allow excess water to drain away. When watered, the compost will retain some water and any excess will drain away. A slow method of applying water is preferable to allow this to take place. It is desirable that the drainage holes do not become blocked either by the compost in the container or by outside material. Old broken plant pots (crocks) can be laid over the drainage holes before the compost is added. This provides a gap through which the excess water can drain. Blockage can also occur if the planter base is flush with the surface it stands on. Recessed draining holes prevent this occurring, or the planter can be slightly raised to allow space for drainage.

The use of broken pots covering the drainage holes prevents blockage as do the recessed holes in this plastic pot.

Watering plants in containers in summer

Remember to continue watering during summer even after periods of heavy rainfall. The wide-leaved foliage of some grasses can act as an umbrella, shedding water off the pot. This also applies when watering a plant from a watering can fitted with a rose. It is much better to lift the foliage at the edge and water direct onto the compost. Apply water at a steady rate, allowing it to soak into the compost. The whole root ball will have received water when it runs from the drainage holes at the base.

Growing space

There should be sufficient space in the container to allow the plant to produce enough roots to sustain growth. Obviously, larger plants will need a large root area. It is possible to grow large plants in containers by following the method and procedure outlined in Chapter 8. However, the container must be of a suitable size to accommodate the plant once it has reached maturity. The shape of the container should also be considered. All containerized plants need to be removed annually for rejuvenation. Some containers have a narrow top and then bulge out lower down. They are not suitable for growing in, because a plant in such a shape will fill the widest part with roots and obviously this will not get past the narrow neck.

Irrigation systems

A wide range of irrigation systems have been developed over the past few years and should be considered if watering containers is a problem due to lack of time or absence from home. Basically, an irrigation system requires a source of water: mains if available, or a reservoir tank using gravity to deliver the water, or tanks connected to the down pipe of your house guttering to collect natural rainwater. From the water source, a simple hose is run to the area in which the containers are situated. Small pipes then run off to each container and end in a jet that delivers the water to the containers when the system is activated. Timer units are fitted that control the frequency and length of time the water is applied. The jets themselves are adjustable so that each pot can receive the correct amount of water for that type of plant.

GRASSES IN CONTAINERS

Grasses without a doubt make excellent subjects for growing in containers. They possess several features that lend themselves to container gardening.

Length of display
With the choice of one of the evergreen grasses, there is some interest throughout the whole year. This will vary as the plant goes through its growing season.

Different colours develop as new growth emerges, seed heads develop, and in some cases autumn tints appear.

Plant form and shape
The grass family being so large, it has a wide range of forms that will suit all situations and container shapes. Vertical statement can be created by using one of the tallish upright grasses. Softer lower areas can be created by using tussock-forming grasses. Because of their growing habit, all grasses form a regular shape. This can be viewed from all sides and the shape is still apparent. This allows them to be used as single specimens in a pot that can be viewed from all sides as you move around the garden. A number of grasses have a naturally arching habit that is lost to some degree when they are planted in the ground. Once elevated by planting in a container, the shape becomes

A range of grasses on Oak Tree Nursery's display at Chelsea 2011. A wide range of forms and shapes, all of which are grown in pots permanently.

more apparent and indeed can increase as the foliage seems to lengthen when it is not restricted by touching the ground. Many of the grasses form seed heads and have fine foliage; with a gentle breeze these move constantly, giving an extra dimension to a planting that few others plants can provide. The very attractive seed heads of a number of grasses may not be fully appreciated if the plant is of medium height; the extra height given by a container often allows the seed heads to be seen against the skyline, when their true beauty becomes apparent.

Rate of growth

Not all grasses are fast-growing. The slower growers are therefore ideal for containers as they can be kept in good-sized containers for many years with just annual maintenance.

Colour variation

The foliage of grasses comes in a wide range of colours and therefore some interesting colour combinations can be created. By careful selection, the colour of the planter can be complemented by the foliage colour, allowing a wide range of container colours to be used to their best advantage. Metal containers are particularly successful when planted up with the blue-foliaged grasses. The brown foliage grasses complement a rust container. Dark corners of courtyards can be brightened by using grasses with white or yellow foliage that will tolerate or indeed like a shady area. Interesting combinations can be created by planting two grasses in one pot. A centre planting of *Imperata cylindrica* 'Red Baron' surrounded by an edging of *Ophiopogon planiscapus* 'Nigrescens' produces a stunning combination.

Site requirements

Grasses have developed to grow in a wide range of environmental conditions; this means that there is usually a grass that will be happy in some area of the garden. For deep shade, the wood rushes (*Luzula* family) are ideally suited. Part shade suits a number of species; *Hakonechloa macra* 'Aureola' does particularly well. In sunny sites, all the silver and blue grasses will be happy, among them a wide range of *Festuca glauca*,

Leymus species and *Helictotrichon sempervirens*. As the grasses are growing in a pot and not the ground, particularly difficult sites that have poor conditions can be improved by standing the potted species in that area as long as the light levels (sunny or shady) are matched to the plant in the container.

Cultural requirements of containerized grasses

The water requirements of each grass will depend on the area from which it originates and so as long as the container is capable of providing that level of moisture, all should be well for good growth. Sedges and reeds will, in general, require more water than other members of the grass family as they originate from moisture rich ground.

One area in which adjustments will have to be made is that of the growing medium (compost) in which the grass is potted. As stated, most grasses prefer a free-draining soil but those that don't (as discussed above) will be helped in their water requirements if the compost used is more water retentive. The addition of water retentive gel mixed in the compost will help as it acts as little reservoirs of water the plant can use as required. A mulch on top of the compost will also assist in reducing evaporation. Various materials can be used dependent on what would suit the pots and garden style. Various coloured gravels, bark chippings, slate, recycled and treated glass are just a selection of materials that are available.

The compost itself is very much a matter of personal preference. As a general rule, most grasses are not restricted to the requirements of an acid or alkaline soil, growing well in the full range, but obviously extremes of each should be avoided. At Oak Tree Nursery, a wide range of compost mixes have been used, from John Innes through to peat based. All were made free-draining with the addition of grit, except for the compost used for moisture loving species. At present, with the understandable concerns with regard to peat reserves, a Coia/bark mix is being used.

The annual care of containers plants and their nutrient requirements are fully dealt with in Chapter 7.

4 Grasses used in a border

The use of the term 'border' usually brings to mind the long and deep borders at country houses, perhaps forming a walk up to the front of the house or along one side of a walled garden. It can, of course, encompass a small border in a suburban garden. Borders usually have a backing of either a hedge or a wall. The front can be straight or have flowing lines, if not heading directly to a focal point. The term is usually preceded by 'herbaceous' as herbaceous plants form the mass of the planting scheme, perhaps with the addition of a few shrubs. The same planting usually applies to domestic gardens but on a small scale. Grasses have been used very little in these schemes, if at all, with the exception of *Cortaderia* (Pampas Grass), planted to give an occasional high point amongst the herbaceous plants.

Gardening, like fashion, goes in trends, however, and in the 1950s grasses came into their own as garden plants to be used alongside herbaceous plants and in their own right. It was mainly due to the work of nurserymen like the Blooms in England, Kurt Bluemel in America and Karl Foerster in Germany that grasses and herbaceous plants are now grown side by side in borders.

Their introduction into plantings on a large scale has revitalized the border, extended its visual impact well into winter and given it additional depth of form and texture. One of the benefits that the use of grasses adds to the overall effect of a border is the lengthening of the season of interest. Traditionally, herbaceous borders would be cut back in autumn, leaving little of interest until the following spring. Many of the taller grasses (*Miscanthus*, *Calamagrostis*, and *Panicum*) don't achieve their full potential until late summer, when most herbaceous flowering plants are on the wane. Use of the coloured-leaved *Miscanthus* ('Zebrinus', 'Cosmopolitan' and 'Cabaret') gives a lift to the border. The graceful seed heads of the flowering *Miscanthus* follow, together with those of the Calamagrostis and then the Panicums. As the season moves into autumn, the grasses start to develop glorious shades of yellow,

red and orange to add to the still attractive seed heads that have now faded to a paler colour.

As autumn moves into winter, the first frosts and the misty mornings arrive and create a whole new effect on the grass stems and heads; although dead, they are still retained in a good, strong, upright statement. These tall groups of grasses can be combined with medium sized evergreens such as *Anementhele lessoniana*, which will add its brilliant autumn/winter colours to the display and, because it is evergreen, will form the basis for the planting scheme right through into spring. The tall perennial grasses can be cut back and the border tidied up during the spring maintenance, when the herbaceous perennials will have started into growth and the border will start to look fully planted again. As the season moves into late spring, the cut-back tall grasses such as the Calamagrostis will be putting up lovely lush green clumps of upright new growth to contrast with the flowerheads of the herbaceous perennials.

The addition of grasses within this herbaceous border has added extra interest, movement and colour in autumn when the herbaceous plants are dying back. The Walled Garden, Scampston, North Yorkshire, England.

OPPOSITE: *Panicum* and *Molinia arundinacea* with *Viburnum* 'Lanarth' in a n autumn extravaganza of colour and form.

If part of the border is in shade, perhaps from an ornamental tree, then the shade tolerant grasses can be used to great effect. *Luzula sylvatica* 'Hohe Tatra' will provide a carpet of evergreen foliage under shade throughout the year. In winter, the lime green leaves start to take on a deep golden yellow colour; this is retained throughout the winter and joined in the spring by brownish-red seed heads held just above the main clump of foliage. *Luzula nivea* starts its flowering period at about this time, with white flower heads standing above dark green foliage with a silver sheen provided by small hairs on the leaf.

The careful choice of flower colours can be used to echo the red/pink plumes of the *Miscanthus*; the white heads of the *Luzula nivea* can be picked up by the daisy-shaped heads of the *Leucanthemum* species; and the white spikes of Veronicas will echo the upright forms of the new seed heads of a number of other grasses. The border, therefore, can have interest for a full year. The wide range of herbaceous perennials also provides an opportunity to choose a selection of plants that can complement each other within one colour band, both in the seed heads and the foliage tones produced throughout the season.

The one feature that grasses bring to a border that no other plant family can, is movement. Most grasses will sway gently with just a small breeze, and for some reason this movement seems to resonate within the person viewing the border. Few people find the gentle movement of a block of fine grasses unpleasing, even if they are not a particular fan of grasses as garden plants. This movement can be amplified by using medium height grasses such as *Stipa tenuissima* and taller species such as *Cortaderia selloana* to carry the movement up and then down again, like a gentle wave moving through the border.

This lightness of plant form that most of the tall grasses possess can be used to good effect in providing high points in the border without the heaviness of form provided by tall shrubs or small trees. The growth habit of tall grasses always forms a spike of slender growth reaching skyward and fading in density towards its tip. This provides a visual high point in the border that is both elegant and structurally strong in moving the eye up and then along to the next focal point, which could easily be the tall flower heads of herbaceous plants.

Traditionally, the edges of herbaceous borders have been formed either by hard landscaped paths or by lawned areas that double as a path. If this edge is straight, it can be difficult to use all the plant space of the border, because plants grow to organic shapes, not straight lines. Some areas will never be filled and have either to be left as bare earth or mulched. Curved border edges are easier to deal with as they conform to the organic shape of the plants. But are these designated paths really necessary? Why not let the plants form the edge themselves by their own shape? The space previously designated as pure path then becomes walking space between two planted borders. It has to be covered with some form of mulch to make a suitable walking surface but this mulch can then be extended into the border, which pulls the whole scheme together in a more flowing and natural shape.

The low-growing plants at the edge of the border can then be allowed to form a more natural shape,

The use of *Calamagrostis bracytricha*, whose seedheads will turn a deeper pink as the season progresses, echoes the pink flowers of the Sedum. RHS Garden Harlow Carr, North Yorkshire, England.

Combinations

Here are some grass and herbaceous combinations used by Neil Lucas at Knoll Gardens in Dorset:

Miscanthus with *Eupatorium*
Molinia caerulea with *Phlomis russeliana*
Pennisetum 'Hameln' backed by *Verbena bonariensis*
Panicum 'Heavy Metal' and *Echinacea* 'Leuchstern'
Molinia caerulea and *Sedum*, especially 'Matrona'
Calamagrostis 'Karl Foerster' and *Verbena bonariensis*
Miscanthus 'Adagio' and *Phlomis russeliana*
Calamagrostis 'Avalanche' and *Sanguisorba* 'Tanna'
Calamagrostis brachytricha and *Persicaria amplexicaulis*

rather than having to be constantly cut back so as not to spill over onto the path; grasses are ideal subjects for this approach. This approach has been carried out by Neil Lucas at Knoll Gardens near Bournemouth and the results totally confirm the credibility and suitability of this landscape method.

The choice of mulch for the path areas will depend to some extent on the beds they surround. Organic materials are best as a mulch on the planted areas, but for a planting scheme in a hot area a mulch of sand and gravel may be more appropriate. This could be extended to the walkway areas, where something like a bark mulch might not look as naturalist. If the planting is under several deciduous trees, a mulch of leaf mould could be applied to the beds.

With the addition of some bark chippings to give more stability and firmness, the pathways could be covered in the same material. This approach makes sense from a horticultural as well as an aesthetic point of view. Organic material will gradually rot down, adding nutrients to the soil, and with a little tidying up and redistribution, the autumn leaf fall can be left more or less *in situ* rather than being collected up and taken away.

A stone/sand mulch has been used on this hot area of planting. The grass-like plant is *Libertia* 'Goldfinger' which prefers a hot, dry site.

In a woodland planting, *Luzula Hohe Tatra* is happy with a mulch of pine needles.

5 Grasses as a one-species planting

In the previous chapter we discussed the use of grasses with other plants to add interest, texture and movement to a planting scheme. This method evolved when grasses were first introduced to the gardener's range of plants; it was not too radical a step away from the traditional approach to designing with plants. As more cultivars were added to the list of species available, grasses gradually started to feature more in planting schemes in the garden as dedicated grass beds, and to be used to a greater degree by landscape designers.

It is perhaps in the area of landscape design that the greatest advances have been made in utilizing grasses to their full potential. Certainly in the UK there is still a long way to go before ornamental grasses are used to their full effect and in their own right, to the extent that they are in the United States. Although the scope of this book is not to discuss large landscape schemes, many of the reasons for using grasses in large schemes can be applied on a small scale for garden plantings.

Where to use one-species planting

Grasses have been used in the UK for hundreds of years as a one-species planting in nearly every public garden space and landscaped area. These grasses are, of course, the specialized varieties used in turf grass. It is perhaps surprising then that we have not thought of using other grasses as a substitute to cover the same areas.

Landscape designers also started to use the tussock-forming grasses such as *Festuca glauca* as substitutes for low-growing shrubs, often in growing conditions of little moisture and in areas difficult to maintain, such as slopes and banks.

Plantings of one species can also be used to create a visual screen or as a defining line between two paths as an alternative to using hard landscaping materials. A screen of grasses is an ideal solution to providing a visual barrier that retains the onlooker's eye in a particular area or that reveals partial views of areas beyond that are not necessarily part of the garden

RIGHT: The one species of *Molinia* 'Poul Petersen', planted at The Walled Garden, Scampston, North Yorkshire, England, to a design by Piet Oudolf. This shows the stunning effect one-species planting can create in a modern style.

OPPOSITE: Modern-style mass planting at the Eden Project in Cornwall.

The use of the upright stems of *Calamagrostis* 'Overdam' combined with *Cornus* creates a visual barrier that still allows view of the lake beyond, at RHS Garden Harlow Carr, North Yorkshire, England.

but add to the visual experience. The required height will dictate what species needs to be used. Most tall species are deciduous but will retain their foliage in a dead form until the next year; this can be an attractive feature in its own right. The previous year's foliage should be cut down in spring, which means that there will be a time gap before the new growth reaches a height sufficient to create a full screen. However, during this time the new foliage does still act as a visual barrier and the fresh colour of the new shoots adds yet another dimension to the garden.

Alternative lawns

Surprisingly, almost all the criteria that lead us to use turf grasses to cover an area can also be met by ornamental grass species. Either by tradition or convention, turf seems to be the preferred option. So what function is it required to fulfil? Fundamentally, we need to cover an area with uniform, low-growing plants, preferably evergreen, possibly to provide a foil or background to a building or feature. It has to be said that on a large scale a properly maintained turf lawn looks superb, especially if it has been designed

Carex flacca can be used as a lawn alternative for light use. Here seen on Knoll Gardens display at the Chelsea Flower Show.

to complement the setting of a historic house. But as we are dealing here with gardens, the factor of scale is not really a consideration. The only function that a lawn provides that an ornamental grassed area cannot is that it can be used for playing sports, a function for which it is ideally suited. Today, many houses have a small lawned area that does not fulfil the sports function and may have originated as a relatively inexpensive way for the house's builder to cover a large area of garden. It could be said that it provides access to other areas. This usually results in a path being worn into the turf, which looks unsightly. Why not make it a permanent path and plant the rest of the area with attractive grasses? Ornamental grasses also have the benefit that a species can be chosen that suits the position and soil of the area. Areas with conditions from shady to hot (conditions that turf grasses struggle with) can be accommodated by the choice of the correct species. Once planted, the ornamental grasses require little maintenance, whereas the turf grass requires cutting as a minimum and if it is to be maintained in top condition also needs watering, aeration and scarifying.

Species and varieties

A good number of grasses are suitable for use as an alternative to turf. The main criteria are that they should be evergreen and low growing, with spreading rootstocks. It has to be borne in mind that the height will always be far greater than that of turf grasses and the finished result will look uneven. If it is thought of more as a 'meadow' than a 'tennis court', the expectations will be met.

Lawn alternatives

Briza media: for light use only
Buchloe: most species
Carex: depending on requirements, certainly *C. praegracilis* and *C. flacca*; light use only
Deschampsia: *D. cespitosa*
Festuca rubra: and its forms
Koeleria: especially *K. macrantha*
Ophiopogon: especially *O. planiscapus*; does not tolerate much foot traffic

Grasses for a screen

Andropogon gerardii
Arundo donax
Calamagrostis × *acutiflora* 'Karl Foerster'
Panicum amarum
Panicum virgatum

Plants should be at a closer spacing than would normally be used, and quick coverage will be obtained if smaller plants are used, as these should grow away into the surrounding area sooner than a mature-sized plant. Until the grasses have covered the total area, bare earth will be visible. The application of mulch will assist in preventing weeds germinating, retaining moisture and adding a decorative background to the new planting. If a path is to be created through the area, then the use of the same material for both the mulch and the path will tie both areas together. Chipped bark would be suitable for woodland areas

The mass planting of *Molinia* 'Poul Petersen' at The Walled Garden, Scampston, North Yorkshire, England, shows how grasses can be used as an alternative to low growing shrubs.

and most temperate gardens. Gravel or crushed stone and sand may fit better into the surroundings in a hot climate.

Grasses as an alternative to shrubs

As previously stated, grasses made an appearance in urban plantings as an alternative to low shrubs. If chosen with care, they can bring a number of features to a scheme that shrubs cannot. Movement is one of the greatest assets of grasses. This is shown to particular effect when they are planted close to and around buildings. The gentle movement of the grass is in complete contrast to the solid and sometimes harsh form of the buildings. Planted in solid blocks of one species rather than split into several varieties, the grasses bring back into the environment the echoes of nature and so soften it. The seed heads produced by many of the grasses offer a delicacy and lightness that

cannot be matched by other plants. Caught by the evening sun, they shine like small jewels and provide a completely different feel to an area. The grasses that produce tall stems topped by seed heads are of particular value as they can soften a harsh wall or fence without the need for a tall plant that can make the area feel enclosed. *Deschampsia* species are excellent for this purpose.

From the maintenance point of view, little is required by grasses. An annual cut back if they are a deciduous species, or a clean over if evergreen, is all that is required. During the time when the grass is not looking its best, it still provides interest and form.

Grasses as a screen

Ornamental grasses can provide an informal screen for most areas of the garden in a range of heights. By its nature, the screening effect will always be informal and is not a substitute for the formal clipped hedge created from shrubs. Nor will grasses produce a feature that will be present all year round as all tall grasses need to be cut down once a year. Having said that, grasses bring to a screen a number of features and advantages that traditional hedging cannot.

From a visual point of view, the grass screen is always soft and changes markedly throughout the season. At the beginning of the season the grasses produce their foliage, which is usually green and fresh in appearance. This is followed by the production of seed heads. These can vary from the pinkish plumes of most of the *Miscanthus* family to the dark brown of, say, *Calamagrostis* 'Karl Foerster'. These seed heads will be retained into the winter, producing yet another colour as they fade to a paler hue. At the same time the foliage is producing a range of yellow, red and brown colours as it moves into the autumnal dying back stage. As grasses will grow to predictable heights, every season it is possible, by choice of species, to have a visual screen of any height, usually incorporating all the previously listed features. It is also possible to create a visual screen that is not solid but is still of a reasonable height. This can be achieved by using grasses that produce seed heads carried high above the basal clump of foliage. *Stipa gigantea* and the *Deschampsia* family all do this. This feature allows views of areas or features beyond the screen to be brought into the overall vista of the garden without becoming overpowering or dominant. It can also lead people into a further section of the garden by tantalisingly showing part of a planting or feature and so arousing people's curiosity to explore further.

With regards to maintenance, the grasses need to be cut back to the base once every year. This is a much quicker and easier operation than trimming back an informal hedge. If the screen is becoming too thick, the grasses can easily be lifted and divided during the annual cutback so that a relatively narrow screen can be maintained. Shrub screening often grows wide and takes up large areas of garden unnecessarily.

A selection of *Miscanthus* varieties are combined here to soften the harshness of a wall. Even in winter the retained dead foliage will provide an attractive screen.

6 Grasses used in a naturalistic planting scheme

Defining a naturalistic planting

The term naturalistic planting can have several definitions, depending on the type of plant to be used. Trees, for instance, can have either a naturalistic shape or what appears to us a formal shape and so the correct species can be selected to fit into and harmonize with the desired feel or concept of the garden. The same can be said of ornamental grasses, for they too have retained many of the characteristics of their native ancestors but by the choice of shape and habit can easily fit into a more formal scheme.

As we are dealing here with ornamental grasses in garden situations, the definition of a naturalistic planting of grasses needs to be defined more exactly. If a grass meadow is desired, the best way to achieve this is to select native species that grow in that situation and sow the whole area. It will then have to be maintained by an appropriate regime to have successful growth. Because of the constraints of area and obtaining the best visual results throughout the year, this particular method of cultivation may not be suitable for a garden, but by the careful selection of ornamental grass species the same effect and feel can be reproduced. Thus the movement, colour tones and textures of a natural grass meadow can be mimicked by using ornamental grasses. Other natural areas that can be adapted to suit a garden situation include woodland plantings and wetland areas.

Prairies and meadows

When aiming to recreate the feel of natural planting, we need to consider where that situation occurs naturally or how it has developed. Climate will have had a major bearing on the species of grass that has established itself in a particular area. It therefore follows that the conditions existing in the garden should be suitable for growing grasses from the natural area you are trying to emulate. If you have a hot site with a free-draining soil, you should be able to create the feel of a prairie, rather than attempting to create an alpine

OPPOSITE: *Nasella (Stipa) tenuissima* used en masse helps link border to wider landscape at RHS Garden Hyde Hall.

milieu or, come to that, an English meadow – neither of which would thrive in the existing conditions.

Plant selection is the next important consideration. When looking at an area of grassland, either in other countries or at home, it may initially seem to be a monoculture, but on closer examination it is usually found that several species have evolved to grow together and exist as one habitat. That habitat is conducive to the growth of the species and as a result the species are usually quite similar in appearance. For instance, in dry conditions you are unlikely to find a broad-leaved fleshy-stemmed plant, as the conditions are not suited to its survival. So when planning an area, this has to be considered. It is quite acceptable to add a different species, to give height or act as a focal point for example; but in order to fit in it must require the same conditions at the predominant planting.

Grasses work best when planted in large numbers to give blocks of shape, form and colour or to give as wide a drift as possible, meandering through other plantings or on their own. Space will dictate the size of planting possible in a garden, but consider incorporating other features such as borders into the grass area to increase the space available. Some herbaceous plants originated in plantings where grass predominated and are quite happy with grasses and add extra interest to them in a garden situation. Select only a small number of grass species to form the predominant planting, especially if space is limited. Three species can offer a surprising range of colours and textures. Or consider using one species as the predominant planting with the addition of, say, three different species to form highlights and features within that planting.

The dictionary definition of a meadow is 'a level tract producing grass to be mowed down'. From this it can be seen that the main difference between a prairie and a meadow is that the former is the natural result of climatic conditions dictating which plants should survive, whereas the latter is man made. The definition of a meadow may also differ. Some people may regard an area of grass with a wide range of flowering plants of differing heights growing within it as a meadow, though this combination might be better described as a wild garden. Others may define a meadow as an area predominantly made up of grasses with a proportion of wild flowers of the same height growing within it. Others may specify that both grasses and flowers should be of native origin. As we are concerned here with creating an area in the garden that has the feel and look of a meadow, some latitude as to plant selection can be tolerated. Because prairies tend to establish in dry climatic conditions, it follows that meadows are more likely to be found in areas with a higher rainfall throughout the year.

As stated previously, meadows are created by human intervention. It may therefore be reasoned that an area of predominantly grass species that has had colonizing trees and shrubs removed is a type of meadow. This may not conform to the common view of meadows as areas of lush grasses with flowers growing among them but it could be regarded as a meadow.

A local nature reserve is such an example, where sheep graze areas of grass at certain times and eat off any saplings that may attempt to grow. This allows a number of native species of grasses and flowers to grow up together. Among all these definitions could

be an area where grass predominates, with some flowering plants growing in it and a reasonable average rainfall, and this, for garden creation purposes, could be classed as a meadow planting as opposed to a prairie planting.

Wetland plantings

The term wetland planting can encompass a number of different planting situations but all of them are based on the presence of water to a lesser or greater degree. At the top of the scale are lakes, ponds and streams, where it is possible to plant directly into water, either into the submerged soil or for smaller features into planting baskets.

The next area of wetland planting is waterside, where the level of water fluctuates during the year. This results in the plants having to accept both submerged conditions for root growth and very wet soil when the water level drops. Furthest away from a body of water are areas that, for the greater part of the year, have wet soil, but during the hot summer months can dry out quite significantly.

Another option is very wet ground, which can be created by dips in the terrain or areas that receive the natural water drainage from other parts of the garden. Happily, the family of ornamental grasses contains plants that will not only tolerate but thrive in all of these conditions. These specimens tend to come from the Sedge, Rush and Reed families, with a small number of true grasses that will grow in some of these wetland areas. In some cases, members of the true grass family can thrive in a situation that would not normally be associated with its natural requirements.

Miscanthus sinensis 'Zebrinus' grows well on the banks of a small stream with fluctuating water levels at Thorpe Perrow in North Yorkshire. Its position is relatively clear of the water for the greater part of the year and yet the site must still be quite wet – not the conditions usually associated with this plant. When planning a wetland planting, it is advisable to follow the recommended requirement of a particular species rather than experiment with positions and conditions not normally associated with that plant. Indeed, the range of forms and colours available for wetland planting is such that it should be possible to find suitable combinations for most situations.

Creating a wetland planting area in a garden that will successfully reflect the wetland areas found in nature is

A naturalistic planting of *Carex muskingumensis* and *Epimedium* give the feeling of a woodland meadow.

perhaps one of the easier areas to achieve. The basis of the area is the body of water and the plantings then follow the different conditions created as the feature moves and blends into the body of the rest of the garden. The only cautionary note is in choosing the species of plant. Due to the sometimes relatively rapid change in their growing conditions, some of the rushes and sedges have developed to cover large areas of ground quickly. Care, therefore, needs to be taken in choosing a species that will not outgrow the size of the area in which it is planted.

Woodland plantings

Two conditions usually accompany woodland plantings: shade obviously, in varying degrees; and dryness, usually caused by the amount of moisture the trees themselves take out of the ground. The majority of true grasses originate from open sunny plains and so do not thrive well in woodland shade. However, there are a number of sedges that have adapted to woodland conditions and so an acceptable and attractive scheme can be created. The varying degrees of shade are important to note. Trees with small leaves and a more open canopy will provide a dappled shade that will make most woodland species quite happy. If this can be combined with an open site where natural light is available from the areas leading up to the woodland, then a wider range of grasses can be successfully grown. The deep shade of large-leaved

trees and conifers provides more of a challenge and reduces the choice of species available. The planning of a woodland area will be dictated in some degree by these conditions; but, in general, large drifts of grasses seem to create a more pleasing scheme when associated with the large scale created by trees. However, for small gardens and correspondingly smaller-scale trees, three or five plants such as the Hakonechloas, which form a wide shape, work very well.

The amount of moisture available also restricts the choice of plants available. If planting under deciduous trees, a grass that grows early in the season is an option. The greater light levels and moisture available before the leaf canopy is produced helps early-growing grasses to thrive. The Melinas and Miliums in particular will exploit this opportunity. A leaf or pine needle mulch may help retain some moisture during hot periods.

Although these general principles are true throughout the world, certain factors can increase the range of grasses grown in shade. For instance, there are higher light levels in the Mediterranean countries and parts of the United States than in the United Kingdom. Combined with warmer temperatures, this will favour species that prefer a free-draining site and enable such plants to thrive. In the UK, they would need an open site to achieve the light and warmth levels needed to grow successfully.

Hakonechloa macra is growing away quite happily under shady woodland conditions. The Walled Garden, Scampston, North Yorkshire, England.

7 Care and maintenance of grasses

By their nature, grasses require little attention throughout the growing season and any major maintenance can be carried out in one operation, usually in the spring.

Specimens grown in pots and containers require a little more attention than those planted in the ground. Growing in pots, they are are divorced from their natural growing conditions such as ample space to spread their roots, natural nutrients in the soil and possibly differing light conditions. Fortunately, being undemanding plants, they can be expected to thrive throughout the growing season once you have provided them with these necessities at their annual maintenance session.

REQUIREMENTS FOR GROWTH

The main requirements for grasses to grow successfully are light, water and nutrients. These basic requirements will be determined by the natural growing requirements of the species. If the plant originates from a woodland environment, its need for a long period of good light will be less than that of a plant that originates on a savannah or open meadow. Therefore, its positioning in the garden, whether as a planted specimen or a potted subject, should be the first consideration in its care.

The same consideration applies to its requirements for the moisture content of the soil, or growing medium if it is a potted subject. Many species that prefer a wet site are quite happy to grow in a range of wet conditions stretching from planted in a pond as a marginal plant to growing in a medium that is moist for at least the majority of the time. However, in that situation, care has to be taken that the compost is moist but not saturated and waterlogged. In the pond marginal planting the plant should be placed in a mesh pot; this allows the roots to move into the water and the exchange of oxygen can take place. In a solid container or in waterlogged ground this cannot

take place and the plant is effectively drowned by the excess water. The varieties recommended for damp or wet areas (see Chapter 10) have evolved in ground with varying amounts of moisture and so they can be grown happily in pots or containers if the same conditions are replicated. If, however, you wish to use grasses as marginal plantings in a pond, you would do well to seek the advice of an aquatic nursery. Although some grasses will tolerate the full spectrum of moisture content, it is best to purchase a plant that has been raised in a water environment and thus grown to accommodate that environment.

As a general rule, most grasses are not greedy for nutrients and will thrive quite happily in a soil that already grows a wide range of plants. Indeed, a soil extremely rich in nutrients could result in excessive growth of foliage. However, some gardeners are under the impression that because the plant is a grass, it will grow anywhere. This is not the case. The native grasses we encounter in our gardens, and would class as weeds, have evolved to grow with the minimum of life-support. Ornamental grasses have been selected for a number of features they possess that make them interesting and attractive in a garden situation. Because grasses are not hungry for nutrients, it follows that they will grow in what might be described as a reasonable soil, but not in a desperate situation such as dry soil that has been sucked dry of moisture, body and nutrients by a leylandii hedge!

MAINTENANCE OF GRASSES IN CONTAINERS

As stated, grasses grown permanently in pots require a little more attention than a garden-grown specimen. This involves a little more ongoing work throughout the growing season and, on reaching maturity, an annual repotting operation.

Ongoing care of grasses in containers

The first consideration when deciding to grow a grass in a container is where the container is going to be placed. The most important factor is the amount of light that will fall on the container. This need not

OPPOSITE: Winter time in the Decennium border with *Miscanthus*, *Panicum* and *Calamagrostis* amongst other perennials.

be direct sunlight, but the minimum requirement is equivalent to the light received at the edge of a tree canopy. This will dictate the range of grasses that can successfully be grown in that container. A location with low light levels or sun for a short time of the day points to a grass that originated as a woodland species. Full sun all day suggests a grass adapted to hot conditions, perhaps with silver foliage to reduce moisture loss.

The next consideration is to provide moisture for the plant. To some extent, the watering requirements will be dictated by the location of the container. A plant chosen to grow in a container in a sunny position should belong to a species that has adopted features that need less water. It must always be borne in mind, however, that a container will not have the same reserves of moisture as the ground and, due to its sides being exposed to the sun and wind, is likely to lose more moisture through evaporation. To compensate for this, some containers have built-in reservoirs of water or allow for water to be retained at the base before any excess is drained off. Gardeners operating in different parts of the world will be aware of how much moisture they need to provide for their plants and there are many varieties of automated watering systems and add-on water reservoirs that can be fitted to containers.

Two simple techniques for moisture retention are worth mentioning and are useful wherever you garden in the world. One is adding moisture-retentive granules to the growing medium; these will absorb moisture when you water and retain it for the plant to use at a later time.

A second technique is to cover the top of the container with a decorative mulch; this helps reduce evaporation of moisture and also enhances the look of the plants (as well as being a weed suppressant). Many varying shades of gravel are available, as well as small pieces of slate or recycled glass for a contemporary look. Chosen with care to complement the planter and the plant itself, they add an extra dimension to any containerized planting scheme. With the exception of the grasses that prefer a moist to wet soil at all times, most grasses will prefer a drier compost to a wet one and most are forgiving if they get a little drier than desired for a short period of time. This makes them a useful plant for containers and, as we should all be mindful of, reduces the use of water in the garden.

The third requirement the gardener must provide for grasses grown in containers is nutrients. There are several ways of providing these, depending on your gardening regime. Fortunately, as stated before, grasses in general require fewer nutrients than most other types of plant. When selecting a growing medium, check to see what, if any, nutrients have been added

to the mix. Usually, if it is a commercially bought pre-mixed medium, the answer is very few or none. Slow-release fertilizer granules are a good way of providing nutrients evenly over a long period. They come in the form of small pellets, the coating of which breaks down over a given period of time, releasing nutrients at a steady rate. They are usually available in either a loose form, looking like pelleted seed, or as a plug formed by sticking the pellets together.

When feeding grasses, if a specific rate for ornamental grasses has not been stated, use half the manufacturer's dose rate for herbaceous plants. This will not change the breakdown period but will provide an appropriate dosage for grasses. Likewise the pelleted plugs can be cut in half or half the dose rate used if more than one plug is recommended for herbaceous plants. The breakdown rates vary from one month to up to a year so a time period can be chosen to suit the gardener's maintenance programme.

Liquid feeds are another way of providing nutrients. These cover a wide range of options. The best choice for grasses is one with a balanced range of major nutrients plus added micro-nutrients. All the ingredients should be listed on the container label. For the organic gardener, liquid feeds can include products such as seaweed and diluted farmyard manures. Again, use at half strength and apply as recommended by the manufacturer.

Annual maintenance of grasses in containers

If all the previous requirements for growth have been met, your grass should be in a healthy condition. The only annual maintenance to be carried out will be repotting as necessary and cutting back or trimming the foliage.

Cutting back the foliage

Two of the most frequently asked questions on the care of ornamental grasses are 'Do I cut it back?' and 'When do I cut it back?' The answer to both these questions applies whether it is grown in a pot or in the garden. Any cutting back of grasses should be done in the spring. Whether you need to cut it back or not requires a little more explanation. As a general rule of thumb, if you look at the grass in the spring and it is all straw coloured, then you can cut it back because all the foliage is dead and the grass is hopefully deciduous. This means it sends up new growth every year which dies off at the end of that same year. If, however, the grass has had a challenging time during the season, say from drought, it may have lost its foliage as a survival mechanism. In this case, you have nothing to lose by clearing those dead stems away in preparation for

Cutting back the dead stems of *Miscanthus* in spring. Secateurs will cut most stems but use loppers on larger specimens.

the new growth that will hopefully appear later in the season.

If when you look at the grass in spring it has still retained the majority of its green growth, this would indicate it is an evergreen species. All that is required is a general tidying of the foliage; in a lot of cases just run your fingers through the plant and the old dead foliage will come away. Other dead foliage can be selectively cut out. For the finer grasses such as the Festucas, an old comb or dining fork can be used to gently comb through the foliage and this usually pulls out any dead material.

Of course, some evergreen grasses have brown foliage and in such plants, only dry straw-coloured material should be removed. The majority of brown-coloured grasses are evergreen. There are, of course, exceptions to this rule but if it is adhered to, the plant should perform well, and once they are experienced, gardeners can enquire and even experiment with cutting back some evergreen specimens to suit their particular gardening regime. The cutting back operation is described fully under 'Care of grasses in the garden' later in this chapter.

Potting on and re-potting containerized grasses

Once a plant has established itself in a container, which usually takes a full growing season, it should be checked every year to see if attention is needed. This attention can take three forms. Firstly, re-potting the plant into a larger container to enable it to grow to its maximum mature size. Secondly, dividing a plant that has filled its container but that you want to keep in the same container. Thirdly, giving attention to a plant that will be staying in the same container for the next growing season. Ideally, it is a good practice to choose a species or variety of grass that will not outgrow the selected container. However, this does restrict the choice of grasses available. Fortunately, most grasses will attain their mature height and characteristics relatively early in their growth cycle, and subsequent growing seasons will see the clump thickening. This means that it is possible to have a grass reaching its mature height and showing its mature features of seed heads in a container narrower than the spread of a mature plant. This can be illustrated by the growing of some of the taller species of *Miscanthus* in pots. In normal garden plantings, most *Miscanthus* attain a height of about 5–6ft with an ultimate base width of about 3–4ft. Growing the plant in a reasonably deep container about 2ft deep, the plant will reach its full height in two to three seasons. Because it is deciduous, the growth should all be cut back in the spring. The new growth it will send up will attain the full mature height and the plant will thicken up its clump by sending up an extra seven or eight new shoots. This process will continue until the plant fills the container and then becomes pot bound. At that stage, the root ball needs to be divided. The root

Newly emerging shoots of *Luzula nivea* in late spring after being completely cut back earlier.

ball will then be much smaller and can be put back into the same container. The space created in that container by dividing the plant allows it to expand into the fresh compost with its new shoots for the next few seasons. As the plant has reached its mature

Two sections can be put back into the pot to grow into one large plant.

Dividing small grasses can easily be accomplished by cutting through the roots with secateurs. For larger, thicker plants, use an old knife or small saw.

height it will continue to do this for the next few seasons until it becomes pot bound again, when the process of division will need to be repeated.

Splitting a containerized grass

Ideally, when splitting a grass you should end up with pieces having equal root growth and shoots. If the growth of shoots has been even it is easy to decide where to divide the root ball to give equal sections. However, if the growth has been uneven and you have several shoots on one side and fewer on the other,

you may need to divide the grass into three sections to obtain an even distribution. Begin by splitting away the largest section. This can then be split again, taking off perhaps a quarter of the section to put with the smaller piece of growth. Ensure you have left enough of the largest piece to make a substantial plant and then carry out the re-potting operation as described below. The remaining two sections can then be put together to form a reasonable plant. Remove any excess root ball so that you can push both pieces together, then any new shoots will emerge close to each other and make compact growth. The sections can then be potted on.

To divide the plant, use a knife to make the initial cut and then gently pull the two sections apart, cutting any thick roots as you go with secateurs. Small plants that are well intertwined can be pulled apart by using two hand forks pushed into the root ball back to back and then levered apart. Large clumps of grasses can be divided by using a pruning saw to cut straight down

Thicker rootballs can be divided by pushing in two hand forks back to back and then pulling them away from each other to start the split. Follow down cutting with secateurs.

the rootball and then dividing the halves into smaller sections if required using the previous methods, or by sawing again if stubborn.

Potting on a grass

Potting on is the term given to the process of moving a plant into the next size container to give it more growing space. Ideally, this should be done before the plant has created so much root that it has formed a solid mass of root ball. Better to have re-potted when it was possible to see some compost between the roots growing around the edge of the root ball. However, if that stage has been passed, it is best to loosen the outside roots away from the root ball. They should come away by easing them with some kind of lever, perhaps a small screwdriver or flat knife blade. Work all around the root ball, including the base, teasing the roots out so that they will grow straight into the new compost. Choose a new container that is the next size up, which should give two to three inches of growing space all around the rootball. There

should be adequate drainage holes in the bottom of the pot. With traditional terracotta pots, this tends to be one large hole in the centre of the base. Pots made from other materials usually have several holes around the base. To prevent the one hole becoming blocked by root growth and compost, it is prudent to put in some crocks. This is usually one or more pieces of broken terracotta pot. Place them over and around the drainage hole. As they are normally curved in shape, they will provide a space between the compost and the drainage hole allowing excess water to drain away.

The plant should be of a depth in the pot to allow a space of about an inch between the top edge of the pot and the top of the root ball. This is obtained by adjusting the level of compost placed in the bottom of the pot. When watering the plant this space allows for sufficient water to be given to it that will then soak down gradually through the root ball. If the space is not left, the water will run over the edge of the pot and be wasted. Fill the space between the root ball and the new pot with compost, gently firming it down as you go round. Make sure the plant is central in the pot and continue with the compost until the top of the root ball is reached. It may be necessary to top up the compost at a later date, as some settling will occur once the plant is watered.

Re-potting a grass

It is possible to keep a grass in the same container for a number of years. If you decide the grass is not quite big enough to divide, you can re-pot it back into its existing pot by carrying out the following measures to provide a little more space for the roots to grow. Ease out the roots from the side of the root ball as described above

Re-potting tips

Mature grasses in large containers can be very heavy and difficult to carry. Lift the container into a large plastic container with handles and then enlist help to carry it to your re-potting area.

Containers with a large central drainage hole have an added advantage when repotting your grass. Loosen the root ball from the sides of the pot with an old knife then, holding the head of a small hammer, insert the shaft through the drainage hole of the pot and push the root ball up. The large pieces of crocks in the base allow the rootball to be pushed out of the container.

To create room for new root growth in a pot, saw off the bottom of the plant about two inches in depth.

and gently scrape away some of the old compost from the root ball. Depending on how much root is present, a space of about an inch can be created around the plant by this process. This will allow new compost to be added into which the plant can grow. The root ball can be reduced further by removing a section of approximately two inches from the base of the root ball. Usually the root is tightly compacted at this point and will have to be cut off. To do this, lay the plant on its side and, using a small pruning saw or old carving knife, cut off the bottom section, just like cutting a slice of bread! Loosen the newly exposed roots and then the plant can be re-potted back into its old container.

CARE OF GRASSES IN THE GARDEN

Annual maintenance

The majority of species require little attention during their growing season, only occasional cosmetic trimming. How much is done depends on the gardener's preference. If dead seed heads are considered unsightly, they can be removed. Follow the individual stems bearing the seed heads down to the base and cut off as near to ground level as possible with a pair of secateurs. This method is preferable to giving the grass a 'hair cut' by cutting off all the seed-bearing foliage at the level of the existing fresh foliage. Although this does remove the offending seed heads,

it leaves behind all the dead, thicker stems, which will detract from the plant's appearance and increase the risk of rotting off.

Likewise, individual damaged foliage or small sections of foliage can be removed in the same way. If you just cut off a blade of grass halfway down, the resulting cut end will turn brown and detract from the overall appearance of the plant.

It is, however, essential to carry out an annual cutting back or cleaning up of garden grown specimens. This should be done in the spring. There are good reasons why it is preferable to leave the dead stems intact over the winter months. Unlike many herbaceous perennials, grasses have a lot to offer to the look of a garden in winter. Some of the evergreen grasses provide excellent autumn colour in their foliage and this lasts into winter. Retained dead foliage still moves in the breeze and adds an element of movement and life to a still winter garden. Tall grasses such as the *Miscanthus* family retain their foliage in its dead form as well as the seed heads and look spectacular covered in heavy winter hoar frost, and again add height to a border when all the tall herbaceous plants may have died back.

This retained foliage also gives some protection to the crown and roots near the surface during the winter frosts. Hibernating insects find the old foliage a safe haven in which to spend the winter, emerging again in the spring before you remove the old foliage.

The best method of cutting back the foliage is to

Cutting back grasses

When cutting back the stems of large grasses such as *Miscanthus*, save the stems. Cut them into short lengths of about 12in (30cm) and tie them together in bundles to form a diameter of about 6in (15cm). These bundles can be placed in dry sheltered spots around the garden and make excellent hibernating sites for over-wintering insects.

The seed heads of many grasses naturally dry out on the plant and will remain intact for several years. They can be used to provide excellent additions to dried flower arrangements indoors.

use a sharp pair of secateurs. Grasses that form thick individual stems, such as the *Miscanthus* family, can be cut back to half an inch from the ground. If you are doing this in late spring, be aware of any new shoots that are showing through as small spear-like projections. These are the foliage for the summer so should not be removed or damaged. Finer grasses can be cut back in the same way, holding a section of the grass in one hand and cutting with the other. This prevents the old foliage falling back onto the plant, making cutting and removal of old growth awkward.

Evergreen grasses will have some damaged foliage that needs to be removed. The low-growing, clump-forming species with wide leaves often have a layer of dead foliage at their base. This is usually removed by firmly pulling the leaf, which should come away at the base of the plant. More stubborn growth can be cut off at the base with secateurs. The fine-leaved evergreen grasses can also have this basal dieback, which usually comes away by pulling. Dead foliage in the heart of the plant can be removed by combing out very fine foliage with an old hair comb or dining fork.

Once the old foliage has been removed, clean away any dead material from the base of the plant to prevent rot setting into the new foliage. If your ground has a poor nutrient content, half the recommended dose of fertilizer can be applied to the soil around the plant. If the plant has grown too large for its position, now is the time to divide it, as described above.

Plants that have been in place for several years may die back in their centre, with all the new growth around the edge making the plant look thin. This can be rectified by lifting the whole plant and dividing the good sections away from the dead centre. These can then be replanted close together to grow into each other and form a new plant. Add a little general-purpose fertilizer to the ground before replanting as the old plant may have taken all the nutrients out of the ground.

8 Pests and diseases

Fortunately, grasses are one group of plants that are not blighted by a wide range of pests or diseases. However, having grown grasses in containers for show purposes for a number of years, the fact that they are containerized and kept in a cold glasshouse for the winter does give some pests the opportunity to colonize the pots or plant as a convenient and pleasant place to overwinter. This also applies to some extent to container plants kept on a patio or around the garden, but the fact that they are subject to winter temperatures will lessen the problem. Annual grasses that have soft foliage may also attract aphids, but these are not usually a problem with the perennial grasses, which have a tougher leaf and are not as rich in sap content as the annual varieties. Even allowing for these examples, pests and diseases are not generally going to be a problem for the gardener. Indeed, some diseases may go unnoticed on a mature specimen growing in the garden and cause so little harm to the overall appearance and growth of the plant that it is not worth applying any treatment. However, the large pests such as mice, rabbits, voles, and deer and, in the United States, gophers can cause considerable damage by eating the newly emerging shoots and digging into the roots to chew them. The damage caused is considerable and has to be dealt with.

Rabbits, mice, voles, deer and gophers

Of these pests, voles are likely to cause the most damage to ornamental grasses, particularly among plantings of low, dense evergreen species similar in habit to the Festucas. This is because in the wild their natural habitat is unkempt grassy areas. They make tunnels through these areas above ground and create a nest between the dense clumps where young shoots of plants and grass are to be found, which they store

RIGHT: Rabbits and hares can eat young shoots. The only acceptable ones are bronze, like this fine pair.

OPPOSITE: The seed heads of *Calamagrostis brachytricha* make an effective screen.

and eat at a later date. There is no deterrent; the only certain solution is trapping. It may be possible to lessen the chance of voles moving into the plantings if the plants are kept clear of old dead grass and are planted near enough to each other to just touch when mature. If surrounding areas of rough grass can be kept to a minimum, this will reduce the chance of voles colonizing the ornamental grass plantings.

If your garden is situated in a rural or even a suburban area, rabbits can cause a great deal of damage in a very short time by grazing the young shoots of low-growing grasses. If rabbits are a persistent problem, the only effective method of protecting large areas of plantings is to erect rabbit-proof fencing. The cost of

this will have to be balanced against the damage caused and its effectiveness once erected if the rabbits can gain access through other areas outside your control, in which case it would be pointless.

Effective rabbit-proof fencing should be constructed of 18 or 19 gauge wire netting with a mesh size of 1 to 1.2in (2.5 to 3.0cm). The fence should be constructed of netting 4 to 5ft (1.25 to 1.5m) deep, of which 12in (30cm) should be buried to prevent the rabbits just digging under the fence, a skill at which they are very adept. Posts and restraining wire should be used to keep the fence from sagging.

If your problem is smaller, selective netting of choice items may be an acceptable solution in deterring individual rabbits or gophers. Mice do not usually present a problem in the garden but may take young shoots if that is all that is available, and in some cases may dig down to eat roots and bulbous root forms. They may, however, cause damage in greenhouses amongst young plants in the spring. As with voles, the only sure remedy is trapping.

Deer fortunately are not a big problem for grasses because the tough, coarse grasses, particularly those with sharp edges, are not to their taste. They may, however, cause some damage to young shoots in the spring. Fencing is the only sure method of prevention, but in most cases the cost is prohibitive.

For all the above pests, various repellent chemicals are available that may act as a deterrent, particularly if the problem is only on a small scale.

Dogs and cats

Dogs and cats can both chew and sit on grasses and owners may find this frustrating. A few rose prunings carefully positioned among grasses may deter cats from reclining and completely flattening the grass. Or why not choose a variety that is not as bed-like in appearance? If all else fails, enjoy the animals relaxing and using the garden. After all, everyone gets different pleasures from a garden, so why not your pets?

Aphids, vine weevil, mealy bugs and scale insects

Aphids can be a problem on annual grasses and occasionally on the young soft growth of perennials. This mainly seems to occur when the plants are kept under glass, as ours are for displaying at shows. Aphids may, however, appear in a warm sheltered garden where other plants can act as their host. Although an aphid infestation is unlikely to damage the grass, it can cause unsightly sooty mould on the leaves from the honeydew the aphids excrete. In light infestations, the aphids can be washed off with a spray of fine water, but for larger infestations a spray with insecticidal soap is a good, environmentally sound control.

Scale insects should not usually be a problem on grasses. However, they may be found on *Acorus* species, which is a grass-like plant although botanically not a grass. The scale insect attaches itself under the leaf, usually on the midrib, and feeds on the sap, again causing an unsightly sooty mould to develop on the excreted honeydew. They can be recognized easily as flat brown scales about the size of a rice grain. The best way to remove them from *Acorus* is to use a mild soap solution and run a sponge from the base of the leaf to the tip. This not only dislodges the insect but also removes the sooty deposits from the leaves.

The vine weevil again should not be a problem

Although not everyone has the pleasure of hens, be aware they love to scratch around in mulches and occasionally like to peck the grasses.

Rust on a sedge, probably brought about by climatic stress.

for outdoor-planted grasses but could be for stock grown in containers. Damage can occur to plants at two stages in the weevil's life cycle. The larvae feed on the roots of plants and the adults eat the leaf, usually indicated by irregular notching on the sides of the leaf. The larvae could cause damage that weakens and possibly kills small immature grass plants but is not likely to affect a mature specimen unless left to multiply to epidemic proportions. The adult can cause a good deal of unsightly damage to mature plants but does not favour true grasses or sedges. They do, however, like *Ophiopogon* species.

Control can be carried out in three ways. Drenching mature plants with a proprietary chemical is very effective. This can be carried out as a precautionary measure if vine weevil damage is noticed on other plant species. This should destroy the larvae, which are small (8mm) and white and live in small cells created in the growing medium. Good garden hygiene is also essential as the adult lives amongst old plant debris during the day.

Mealy bugs can be a more serious problem but are not commonly found. They are small (4mm long) creatures that live in the base of the plant, usually hiding between the leaf sheath and the stem. They cover themselves in a white powder, which is all that will be seen. The first indication of mealy bugs could be stunted growth of the plant and, on close inspection, white powder covering the base and lower leaves of the plant. Light infestations on small plants can be treated by proprietary sprays but because of the bug's favoured position, the sprays may not reach into all

parts of the plant where mealy bugs are present. In such cases, the only option is to remove and burn the infected plant. Fortunately the mealy bug cannot spread over large areas and is usually confined to a few feet around a host plant. Bringing in infected stock is usually the way in which the problem is introduced and careful observation of the health of all new plants can avoid the problem.

Slugs and snails

For most of the grass family these two creatures do not present a problem. However, plants with soft wide leaves, such as *Carex siderosticha*, can be a target. If there is already a problem with slug and snail damage on other plants, it is perhaps best to choose another species of grass. Partial control can be achieved by hand-collecting the creatures at night but this has to be maintained and is not by any means an absolute control.

Rust

A more common problem for a number of grasses can be rust. This is a fungal disease that manifests itself in the form of small orange-rust coloured spots on the leaf or browning sections of the leaf. As rust is a fungus, it does respond to fungicide treatments. Other cultural methods that can be employed to reduce or avoid an outbreak are to allow plenty of air flow between the plants and practise good garden hygiene by cleaning up any dead material with rust on.

9 Acquiring grasses

BUYING PLANTS

With the popularity and use of grasses in gardens increasing, the ways in which the gardener can obtain plants have also increased. To some extent the way plants are purchased will be governed by the size of scheme intended and the financial constraints on the gardener. The options open to gardeners are either to buy in plants from a commercial source or produce them themselves from seed or division of existing plant stocks.

Grasses from commercial outlets will come in two forms: containerized or bare root.

A containerized stock will have been raised in a nursery to the point at which it can be planted out into the garden as a viable plant. The nursery trade grades its pot sizes by centimetres for smaller pots, for example 9cm and 11cm, which is the measurement of the top of the pot sides, but for larger pots, it is measured by volume size, for example 1 litre, 2 litre and so on. Depending on the growth habit of the plant, choose the appropriate pot size. A *Miscanthus*, for example, is a big grass; it will be larger as a young plant and therefore require a correspondingly large pot from the start. A *Festuca*, on

the other hand, will not make a large plant on maturity and therefore only needs a small pot in which to reach a saleable size. Therefore, it does not follow that a large pot means that an older and more mature plant is being purchased.

Bare root-stock means that the grass has been grown in a field and is lifted and sold in its dormant season. The plant will have no soil attached to the

RIGHT: Young plants at various stages of production. Raised at a local nursery, they will be acclimatized to local weather conditions.

OPPOSITE: *Stipa gigantea* seed heads add to the effect of a herbaceous border in late summer at Scampston Walled Garden, Yorkshire.

Carex morrowii 'Ice Dance'. On the left, a 9cm pot, and on the right an 11cm pot. The 11cm plant would be about twice the age of the 9cm size.

roots and all its dead foliage will have been removed. To those unfamiliar with buying stock in this way, this can look quite alarming, but as long as the root-stock has not been allowed to dry out, the plant should grow away well in the next season.

Where to buy grasses

There are two types of outlet for purchasing grasses. One is direct from the person who has grown them. This is usually at the nursery or at a plant fair or garden show. Plants can also be obtained at garden centres or other outlets that have a garden section. In this case, the plants are likely to have been bought in from growers or may have been raised in-house. Plants may also be bought by mail order or on-line from either of these sources.

It would be unfair to say that one is better than the other as both have advantages. Buying direct from the nursery usually means that you will be dealing with the person who has grown the plant and so will be able to give expert advice on its requirements. There is also

Grass plants available at an RHS flower show. A wide range of species are usually available sold by the nursery where they were raised.

likely to be a wide range of plants available at a nursery that specializes only in grasses. However, you may have to travel some distance to find specialist nurseries.

Garden centres are located in all areas and are easily accessible, but may not stock the range of grasses and may not have the grower's specialized knowledge. Some garden centres, however, have developed a good grass section and do have qualified staff to assist in enquiries.

If buying by mail order or on-line care must be taken to determine the size of the plant being offered and in some cases the hardiness of that particular species for the area for which it is intended.

What to look for

If purchasing containerized stock, it can be planted at any time of the year because it will have a good root system. However, if an option is available it is best to purchase in spring when most grasses are making new growth. Some nurseries like to offer a more mature plant, which will be in a larger pot. Although this may initially give the impression of a fuller garden bed, in the long term the difference in size may be minimal. Younger plants in smaller pots will often put down more root to establish themselves. This growth may be more rapid than that of a mature plant, which will have put down sufficient root to sustain itself and does not need to expand as quickly. In the next couple of seasons, the young plant may catch up with the mature plant. Whatever the choice, the following points should be looked for when buying containerized stock.

- The plant should comfortably fill most of the pot and not be a small plant in the middle of a large pot. If it is, you may be paying for a pot of compost rather than a plant.
- The plant should not be pressing on all sides of the pot with no signs of compost between the plant and the pot. This would suggest that the plant is pot

bound – its roots have formed a solid mass that has to be cut away to allow new growth. The plant may not have been able to take up sufficient nutrients and water and so may be in a stressed state.

- The foliage should look healthy and not show signs of rust or fungal disease. If deciduous, the old foliage should have been cut away, so look for signs of new growth coming through.
- Every plant should be labelled with the species and variety. Check the variety is the one you want. Miscanthus, for instance, grow in a wide range of heights. Don't end up with a dwarf plant when you want a tall plant.
- If buying annuals in pots, purchase early in the year before the inflorescences are showing. The plant can then grow away in the garden and will probably flower much more quickly. If you wait until the plant is in flower, you will only have it for a short period before it dies.

INCREASING STOCK BY SEED AND DIVISION

All species of grasses and their botanical varieties come true from seed collected from the mother plant. This makes them ideal candidates for gardeners to increase their stocks of plants for planting up large areas.

For annual grasses, growing from seed is the only option, either by purchasing from a seed company, or by taking seed from last year's plant. Indeed, if the original plant is producing seedlings in the area required by the gardener, it may be the best option to let nature do its work by self-seeding. Any unwanted seedlings in the wrong areas can be weeded out. If, however, the annuals are to be used as part of a specific bedding or planting scheme, then plants raised in containers would be the best option.

Named cultivars should be increased by division of a good representative of the cultivar, thus ensuring that the notable characteristics of that cultivar are carried on.

Raising grasses from seed

The grass seed is essentially a package containing the embryo of its parents and enough food reserves to carry it through its establishment stage, all enclosed in a seed case for protection. For the gardener experienced in raising plants from seed, the process of producing annual grasses from seed is outlined in Chapter 2. This process also applies to perennial grasses.

For the less experienced, the process is explained a little more fully here. For a seed to germinate, it needs moisture, light and warmth. Most grass seeds will germinate quite happily in natural light at a time of year when the air temperature begins to rise, which is usually spring, and this is the best time to sow. If plants are needed earlier and the light is sufficient, a well-sited glasshouse will usually have sufficient light and a little bottom heat from a propagator will trigger the germination process. Seed can be either bought from a commercial source or collected from plants the previous season. Quite a number of garden plants need some form of pre-germination process but, happily, most grasses do not. The seed should be collected as it becomes ripe and before it disperses. This is usually quite easy to judge with grasses as the flowers will start to turn brown as they dry. Periodically shake or run the seed head through your fingers and as soon as the first seeds are ripe, they will come away in your hand. The whole head can be harvested and allowed to dry indoors if required. Cut off the grass flower heads and bunch them together. Place them seed head downwards in a paper bag and lightly tie the neck of the bag round the grass stems. The bag should then be left in a dry, airy place for the seed to ripen. Shake the bag occasionally and the ripe seeds will fall to the bottom of the bag. Moisture is the one thing to avoid as the seeds can turn mouldy and rot off. Collect and store grass seeds in paper bags because plastic can cause condensation. The collected seed can then be stored until the following spring in a cool, dry place which is free from the attentions of mice. Don't forget to label the packet as it is impossible in most cases to guess the variety of grass from the seed.

Depending on the amount of seed collected or the number of plants required, a suitable container can be chosen, either a pot, tray or modules. The container should be big enough to allow the seedlings

Terms used in propagation

Bottom heat: the warmth in a propagator normally provided artificially from under the compost to encourage germination and growth.
Capillary action: the process by which water will rise above its normal level through a series of very small spaces, for instance, in compost.
Compost: a soil substitute for propagating and establishing plants. Different types are formulated to meet the plant's nutrient and moisture requirements at a particular stage in its life.
Germination: the first stage in the growth of a seed into a seedling.

sufficient room to develop to the stage when they are big enough to prick out. With grass seeds, several individual plants are clumped together to grow into one plant. Because of the shape of the leaf, they can be sown a little closer together than other plants that produce a large seed leaf that, if touching others, could cause rotting off or damping back.

The compost used should be a specialized seed compost that has been formulated to meet the needs of seedlings. It will be finer in composition than potting compost and contain fewer nutrients. The choice of compost is entirely personal as long as it is formulated for seeds. It can be either peat based or any other alternative. The chosen container can then be filled with compost in preparation for sowing. The only difference between module trays and pots or seed trays becomes clear when the seedlings are ready to be pricked out. With modules, a few seeds are sown in each individual cell and allowed to grow together to form one plant that is then potted on into an individual larger pot to grow. Modules reduce the amount of root disturbance as the whole section is pushed out from below and potted on. However, care needs to be taken at the sowing stage that not too many seeds are put in each module as this can lead to weak growth or damping off. As grass seeds are small, it is easier to achieve a more evenly spaced sowing in a pot or tray, although some root disturbance will be unavoidable when pricking out. One method is not superior to the other, so it really depends on individual preference.

The aim when preparing a container for seeds is to provide a flat, firm surface with sufficient depth of compost for good root growth during the early stages of the plant's life. A depth of about 5cm is adequate. The process for filling pots and seed trays is the same.

Fill the container with compost until it is heaped slightly above the rim. To remove any air pockets, gently firm the compost into the corners and down to the base using fingers only. The compost should not be compacted. Remove the excess compost by running a board along the top edge of the container using a sawing action and running the full length of the container. To firm the compost, use a presser board (a board cut slightly smaller than the container but which will fit into the corners). Press gently down to form a firm and level seed-bed. A space of about 10cm should be left between the seed-bed and the top of the container. To ensure the compost has enough moisture for the seeds, stand the seed tray or pot in a larger container of water so that the level of the water comes halfway up the side of the seed container. Water will then pass through the compost by capillary action. The compost will turn a darker colour when fully soaked and then it can be removed

A selection of seed trays, pots and modules. Choose the appropriate one depending on the number of plants required to be grown.

Tray filled with compost, air pockets removed by gentle firming with fingertips.

Using a sawing motion, remove any excess compost from the top of the tray.

The firmed seedbed in the tray and pot ready for sowing the seeds.

Two pots of *Luzula nivea* seedlings ready to be pricked out into individual pots. On the right, a young plant three weeks after pricking out.

small, fine dry sand can be added to them to make the distribution more even. Finally, lightly cover the seeds with vermiculite or very finely sieved compost. As a general rule, a depth the same as that of the seed is sufficient. Label the seed container with the variety and date. The air temperature in spring should be sufficient to start germination so leave the seeds in a light area. A piece of glass can be placed over the tray to keep moisture and temperature even but this should be turned daily to prevent condensation forming.

As soon as the seeds break the surface of the compost, raise the glass slightly to let more air circulate and then remove it completely after a couple of days. For most grass seeds, a germination time of about fourteen days can be expected. The compost should be kept moist by spraying with a hand sprayer or a small watering can with a very fine rose. Care should be taken to keep the seedlings out of fierce direct sunlight and do not water at the hottest time of the day as this can cause scorching or burn them off.

The next stage is to prick out the seedlings into individual pots to grow on. At this stage, the seedlings should resemble a fine lawn and be about 15mm tall. Small pots about 6cm are a good size for pricking out the seedlings. Use a proprietary seedling compost and fill the pots so that the compost is just over the rim. Strike off the compost level with the rim and then gently press it down to leave a small gap to allow watering to take place during the growing on of the plant. The aim is to gather a small group of individual seedlings together to form one plant. In the compost of the new pots, make a hole sufficiently large to accommodate the roots of the grass seedlings. Lightly hold the tips of a small group of seedlings and using a dibber or seed label lift up the roots of the group from below. Supporting the roots, transfer the group to the prepared pot and lightly firm around the seedlings, trying not to disturb the group. When a large enough batch has been lifted from the seed tray to their new pots, water them in using a fine rose and leave in a warm environment to re-establish a good root growth. Keep moist but take care not to let the compost become waterlogged by over-watering.

If growing in module trays, the clumps of seedlings are extracted by pushing from below the root with a dibber or pencil and then potting on as for the pot-raised seedlings.

Grow the plants on in a warm environment until a good root ball has been established. They can then either be potted on into the next size pot and put outside to grow on, or, if they have made enough growth, planted out into their permanent beds.

from the water and left on a bench to allow excess water to drain out of the holes in the base of the container.

When sowing the seeds, the aim is to distribute them evenly over the whole area. They can either be shaken out of the packet or sown in small lots picked up between two fingers and a thumb and sprinkled evenly until all the compost is covered. Keep the seeds close to the compost so they do not bounce to other areas. Because most grass seeds are quite

A modular tray with seedlings at a stage ready to be potted on.

Division

Named cultivars should be reproduced by division. The process of division is very simple and just consists of splitting a plant into pieces or small clumps, each with a reasonable amount of root. With the smaller grasses this is easily accomplished by hand, but for the larger specimens the use of a hand tool such as a saw or fork may be required to separate small enough pieces to pot up. While most grasses are happy to be divided, a few such as *Stipa gigantea* do not like the disturbance this involves. However, this can be avoided by just taking a slice out of the side of the plant whilst it is in the ground, thus avoiding the disturbance of lifting the whole plant. It is best not to be too greedy and only take out a few pieces of reasonable size, say 10cm wide, and these will stand a much better chance of survival than many smaller pieces.

As a general rule, the best time to divide grasses is in the spring when they are just coming into their growing season. This is particularly true with deciduous varieties and coincides with their cutting back as part of the annual maintenance. Evergreens can be divided at any time of the year but it is probably best to avoid the very hot period of midsummer and the colder time of winter. If the grass is in active growth it stands a much better chance of re-establishing itself during favourable growing conditions of warm temperatures and some rainfall. Once the original plant has been divided, the new plants can either be replanted straight away into a newly prepared bed or grown on in a pot to be used at a later date. If using pots, choose a size to allow enough growth in the next season to avoid

A plant divided into two new plants ready to be potted on individually.

disturbing the plant again. Choose a proprietary potting compost that will contain some nutrients but do not give additional feed at this stage. Ensure the new plant does not dry out during hot weather as it will not yet have established a large root system.

10 Selecting the right grasses

The key factor to any planting scheme, whether containerized or in a garden setting, is to choose the species that suits your conditions. This will ensure healthy growth and a successful effect in the garden. In this chapter, which is a checklist of grass species, the grasses are arranged in groups firstly by their mature height, since this is probably the first factor to be borne in mind when choosing a grass. The given heights are what can reasonably be expected from the grass, but this may vary depending on the situation in which the plant is placed. This is followed by the required growing conditions, which will affect the ultimate height of the plant and its health and vigour. Given the wide range of conditions and environmental factors that can come into play, it is impossible to give a definite description for each site. This means that a grass that prefers a hot sunny site may grow satisfactorily in a part shade area but probably not in a damp area because, coming from a sunny climate, it will probably be used to dry soil conditions. The groupings, therefore, are designed more as a useful guide to what can successfully be grown in those conditions, but definitely not a definitive set of undeviating requirements.

The selection of what grasses to include has been based on a range of species that have been used in gardens for a considerable time and can therefore be relied upon to perform as stated. They are also varieties that can be recommended with confidence from personal experience, though inevitably this may result in some excellent varieties being left off the list not because they are not garden worthy, but because they do not fit into the chosen categories.

Hardiness is always an unpredictable factor to judge. How the plant reacts to a cold winter may depend on how it has fared in the past growing season. The winter of 2010/2011 started with an early frost in many places in the UK. This, combined with a harsh winter the previous year and heavy rainfall, resulted in some plants failing that had previously been considered hardy. It can only be said that given normal winter conditions, the hardiness zones are correct. Hardiness zone maps are available, but a table of minimum temperatures may be a more reliable guide due to the enormous variations that can occur in local temperature.

Minimum temperature (Celsius)	Zone	Minimum temperature (Fahrenheit)
Below −45	1	Below −50
−45 to −40	2	−50 to −40
−40 to −35	3	−40 to −30
−35 to −29	4	−30 to −20
−29 to −23	5	−20 to −10
−23 to −18	6	−10 to 0
−18 to −12	7	0 to 10
−12 to −7	8	10 to 20
−7 to −1	9	20 to 30
−1 to 4	10	30 to 40
Above 4	11	above 40

TALL GRASSES

A selection of grasses that will be above 4ft (120cm) high at maturity.

Tall grasses for a hot site

Andropogon gerardii Big Bluestem, Turkey Foot (grass)
Height: Europe 4ft (1.2m) to 6ft (1.8m); USA southern limit of Oklahoma 3ft (90cm), eastern limit of Colorado 10ft (3m).
Spread: 2ft (60cm).
Hardiness: Zone 5.
Deciduous.

Upright silvery-blue stems with arching blue leaves. Good late summer/autumn colour of reddish hue to tips of leaves, turning to rich red and purple during autumn. Flower plumes produced in late summer to early autumn, carried on slender stems often in threes, resembling the toes on a turkey's foot, hence the common name. Tiny red anthers hang down. Clump forming.

OPPOSITE: The interesting foliage of the Panicum family can be used to good effect in many areas of the garden.

Arundo donax Giant Reed, Provencal Reed (grass)
Height: Europe 15ft (4.5m); USA, north-eastern 14ft (4.2m); warm regions 18ft (5.5m).
Spread: Clumper in cool gardens but will spread rapidly by rhizomes in warm climates.
Hardiness: Zone 6.
Semi-evergreen.

Old-established grass (1648) to England from Southern Europe. The tallest hardy grass. Upright hollow stems bear coarse grey leaves that can be 3in (7.5cm) wide, borne 6in (15cm) apart at right angles. Flowers with large fluffy panicles 12in (30cm) long but only in warm climates, hence seldom flowers in Britain. Stems used for wind instruments.

Arundo donax (Provencal reed) – probably the tallest blue grass.

***Arundo donax* 'versicolor'** (or **'variegata'**)
(Striped Giant Reed)
Height: Europe: 5ft to 8ft (1.5 to 2.4m); USA shorter than species grown in same location.
Hardiness: Zone 6 in USA. Needs sunny, protected site in Britain.

Stunning variety with cream and green striped leaves that age to a yellowish white. Makes a dramatic subject grown in containers.

***Calamagrostis* × *acutiflora* 'Avalanche'** Reed Grass (grass)
Height: Europe 4ft to 5ft (1.2 to 1.5m); USA 5ft (1.5m).
Spread: Clump forming to about 3ft 3in (1m).
Hardiness: Zone 4.

A new selection of *Calamagrostis* 'Karl Foerster'. Inherits the tall upright growth of its parent with a white band down the centre of its leaf and silver plumes that appear early summer.

Calamagrostis x acutiflora 'Karl Foerster' (Feather reed grass) Even in winter the seed heads are attractive on the skyline.

***Calamagrostis* × *acutiflora* 'Karl Foerster'**
Feather Reed Grass (grass)
Height: Europe 4ft (1.2m); USA 5ft (1.5m).
Spread: Clump forming to about 1m but very tight grouped stems.
Hardiness: Zone 4.
Deciduous.

A garden-worthy grass by any standard. Dark green foliage is produced in spring and lasts all season. Vertical flower stems are produced in July to August and are open and feathery with a purplish tint. These turn to narrow upright plumes in late summer and then to a lovely buff colour. Height about 6ft 6in (2m). An excellent grass that gives good vertical accent to borders and retains its upright growth throughout the season without the need for support. Looks particularly effective in a container.

Calamagrostis emodensis. Elegant buff-coloured heads move gently with the slightest breeze.

Calamagrostis emodensis (grass)
Height: 4ft to 5ft (1.2m to 1.5m); USA 1.5m (5ft).
Spread: Clump forming. Large clumps of bluish green leaves to about 3ft 3in (1m) wide.
Hardiness: Zone 5.
Deciduous.

Nice clump-forming foliage from which emerges numerous fluffy pendulous green flower heads that turn beige with age but are retained on the plant throughout the season. These can be cut and remain intact for flower arrangements. Leaves emerge early summer followed by flowers in late summer. Likes a free-draining site.

Calamagrostis acutiflora 'Overdam' (Striped feather grass). The pinkish seed heads turn to straw brown and are retained well into winter.

Calamagrostis × acutiflora 'Overdam' Striped Feather Grass (grass)
Height: Europe and USA 3ft 3in (1m).
Spread: Clump forming to about 3ft 3in (1m).
Hardiness: Zone 4.
Deciduous.

Similar to 'Karl Foerster' in growth habit but has cream to white striped foliage which fades slightly through the season. Its flower plumes are tinged pink and are produced in late spring to early summer.

Chondropetalum tectorum (restio)
Height: Europe and USA 3ft 3in to 4ft (1m to 1.2m).
Spread: A very tight clump up to 1m wide.
Hardiness: Zone 8.
Evergreen.

Rich dark green stems with dark brown flowers on the tips. Originating from South Africa, it makes an excellent feature plant. The stems arch out from the base to form a clump, eventually touching the ground. Makes an excellent container plant.

Cortaderia Richardii Toe Toe, Tussock Grass (grass)
Height: Europe and USA 10ft (3m).
Spread: 10ft (3m).
Hardiness: Zone 8.
Evergreen.

Originating from New Zealand, this is a fabulous feature plant, although must be given the room required. Sending up tall upright stems from the centre of the plant, they arch in all directions. The inflorescences are not as fluffy as the other pampas grasses but they are the more attractive. Bronzy gold in colour when first produced in mid to late summer, they fade to cream. If intended for flower arranging, they should be cut just before fully open. The base can accumulate a lot of dead foliage and it is best cleaned out annually but care should be taken as the leaves can cut and thick gloves should therefore be worn.

Cortaderia selloana (Pampas grass). A traditional old favourite used widely by the Victorians as accent plants in borders. Sharp foliage, soft seedhead.

Cortaderia selloana **'Pumila'** Pampas (grass)
Height: Europe 5ft (1.5m); USA 6ft 6in (2m).
Spread: 5ft (1.5m).
Hardiness: Zone 5.
Evergreen.

A native of Brazil, the family of pampas grasses has obtained a reputation for outgrowing gardens and being difficult to manage. This is the fault of gardeners planting the larger varieties in too small a space. 'Pumila' is a medium-sized variety and therefore suits domestic gardens better. Its plumes are white in colour, produced in late summer and held upright from the centre of the plant. They will last over winter to be cut out in spring when the base of the plant should be cleaned out of any dead foliage. Beware, the leaves can cut your hands quite easily and thick gloves should be worn.

Cortaderia selloana **'Sunningdale Silver'** Pampas (grass)
Height: Europe and USA 10ft (3m).
Spread: 5ft (1.5m).
Hardiness: Europe Zone 5; USA Zone 8.
Evergreen.

The archetypal pampas grass beloved of the Victorians, this variety was introduced before 1938. Needs plenty of space to spread out to its full size and produce its magnificent plumes, which are whitish silver in colour and produced late summer. This variety is held to be the best for size and grandeur. Care to be taken when removing the leaves as again, they are very sharp and can cut your hands.

Cortaderia selloana **'Splendid Star'** Pampas (grass)
Height: Europe 3ft to 4ft (90cm to 1.2 m); USA 4ft (1.2m).
Spread: 3ft 3in (1m).
Hardiness: Zone 5.
Evergreen.

A dwarf variety of pampas. Gold-streaked leaves and white plumes. A good plant for containers, giving all the shape and style of the larger pampas grasses.

Miscanthus × *giganteus*
Height: Europe and USA 10ft (3m).
Spread: 4ft (1.2 m).
Hardiness: Zone 4.
Sunny site; deciduous.

As the name implies, one of the tallest Miscanthus. Dark, wide foliage forms a pendulous clump. Occasional pink flowers in colder climes. Best used as a screening grass or for large massed foliage effect.

Miscanthus nepalensis
Height: 4.5ft to 5ft (1.4m to 1.6m).
Sunny, well-drained site; deciduous.

An unusual looking *Miscanthus*, having goldish drooping flower plumes not unlike tassels of golden cord. These are held well above the mound of light green foliage. A very delicate-looking plant that, although hardy, will require a sheltered site in wetter, colder climates.

Miscanthus purpurascens Autumn Flame Miscanthus
Height: Europe and USA 5ft (1.5m).
Spread: 4ft (1.2m).

Hardiness: Zone 4.
Sun or part shade; deciduous.

This variety does not flower readily but has excellent foliage colour, green turning to orange and red tints from late summer onwards. Open in habit. Stems attractive and reddish purple in colour.

Miscanthus sacchariflorus Silver Banner Grass
Height: Europe and USA to 10ft (3m).
Spread: Will continue until contained.
Hardiness: Europe Zone 7; USA Zone 4.
Sun or part shade; deciduous.

A very large Miscanthus useful for making a bold foliage statement. Bamboo-like stems with wide bright-green leaves. Spreads slowly and is not invasive but will require a large space to grow into. Rarely flowers in the UK.

Miscanthus sinensis

Found in Japan, Korea and China, this is a very popular family of grasses much cultivated. Typically they produce upright stems bearing a leaf with a whitish midrib 1in (25mm) wide and a flower plume, which is quite slender and ranges from red when young to very pale brown or white. Growth habit is clump forming. Although deciduous, they retain their dead foliage on the stems throughout the winter months, which can be attractive in its own right in the garden. There are a wide range of cultivars available offering different heights, winter colour and flowering times. The following list is just a selection of those widely available and the second list is a selection of garden-worthy varieties that may take a little more finding but are well worth the effort.

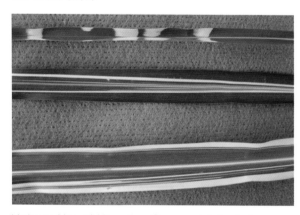

Variegated leaved Miscanthus. Grown mainly for their decorative leaf colour, they all flower occasionally. From top to bottom: Miscanthus Zebrinus (Zebra grass), Miscanthus 'Cabaret', Miscanthus 'Cosmopolitan'.

Miscanthus sinensis var. condensatus 'Cabaret' (grass)
Height: Europe 7ft (2.1m); USA 9ft (2.7m).
Spread: 4ft (1.2m).
Hardiness: Europe Zone 7; USA Zone 6.
Deciduous.

Of all the Miscanthus species grown for their foliage, this is probably the most striking. The leaves are 32mm wide when mature and are dark green with a creamy white centre and borne on upright stems. 'Cabaret' produces a flower but needs a warm growing season of considerable length, which it does not always receive in the UK, therefore it seldom flowers to any notable effect. However, the foliage and upright growing habit make it well worth a place in the garden.

Miscanthus sinensis var. condensatus 'Cosmopolitan' (grass)
Height: Europe 7ft (2.4m); USA 10ft (3m).
Spread: 4ft (1.2m).
Hardiness: Europe Zone 7; USA Zone 6.
Deciduous.

The reverse of the colouring of 'Cabaret', being creamy white with a green centre, although the colours may not be as deep as 'Cabaret'. Similar upright habit but flowers more frequently, having coppery red flowers in late summer.

Miscanthus sinensis 'Ferne Osten' Far East (grass)
Height: Europe and USA 4ft (1.2m).
Spread: 3ft 3in (1m).
Hardiness: Europe Zone 7; USA Zone 6.
Deciduous.

This variety has very dark red flower plumes in mid to late summer and excellent winter foliage colour, being upright and copper and red. A very popular variety for smaller gardens, being just 1.2m in height.

Miscanthus sinensis 'Flamingo' (grass)
Height: Europe 5ft (1.5m); USA 6ft 6 in (2m).
Spread: 4ft (1.2m).
Hardiness: Europe Zone 7; USA Zone 5.
Deciduous.

The flower heads are slightly pendant and more open than other varieties. Flowering late summer, the plumes are dark pink in colour fading to whitish brown. Good autumn foliage colour.

Miscanthus sinensis 'Gracillimus' (grass)
Height: Europe 6ft (1.8m); USA 7ft (2.1m).
Spread: 5ft (1.5m).
Hardiness: Europe Zone 7; USA Zone 5.
Deciduous.

Introduced from Japan around 1878, this is one of
the earliest forms and still one of the best. Noted for
its round form and fine foliage, it flowers late in the
season (late summer) and has copper-red plumes that
fade to silver white. However, it does require a long,
warm growing season and therefore does not always
give a large show of flower plumes in England. Its
leaves turn pinky orange in autumn and then fade to a
straw colour for winter.

Miscanthus sinensis 'Graziella' (grass)
Height: Europe 6ft (1.8m); USA 6ft 6in (2m).
Spread: 4ft (1.2m).
Hardiness: Europe and USA Zone 5.
Deciduous.

An upright variety with silver flower plumes carried
high above its foliage and opening late summer. The
foliage has good winter colour of rich copper red and
orange.

Miscanthus sinensis 'Kleine Fontane' (grass)
Height: Europe and USA 5ft (1.5m).
Spread: 4ft (1.2m).
Hardiness: Zone 5.
Deciduous.

Narrow leaves. Flower plumes are reddish purple
fading to silver pink, erect in bud then becoming
pendulous later. Foliage fades to beige in the autumn.

Miscanthus Malepartus. The deep red seed heads eventually turn buff and become fluffy.

Miscanthus sinensis 'Malepartus' (grass)
Height: Europe 6ft (1.8m); USA 7ft (2.1m).
Spread: 4ft (1.2m).
Hardiness: Europe Zone 7; USA Zone 6.
Deciduous.

Broad green foliage with magnificent show of flower
plumes that are held well above the foliage, dark red in
colour, fading to silver. Autumn foliage colour purplish
then orange and red. Flowers early summer in England.
One of the best *Miscanthus* varieties.

Miscanthus sinensis 'Rotsilber' (grass)
Height: Europe and USA 5ft (1.5m).
Spread: 4ft (1.2m).
Hardiness: Europe Zone 7; USA Zone 5.
Deciduous.

A compact variety with bright green foliage. Flower
plumes are deep red in summer fading to silvery pink.
Good autumn colours of orange and red and many
flower heads.

Miscanthus sinensis 'Strictus' Porcupine Grass
(grass)
Height: Europe 6ft (1.8m); USA 9ft (2.7m)
Spread: 2ft 2in (75cm)
Hardiness: Europe Zone 7; USA Zone 5.
Deciduous.

Miscanthus Zebrinus (Zebra grass). One of the first garden-introduced *Miscanthus*, but still garden worthy.

Another older *Miscanthus*, introduced in 1904. Very upright foliage with bands of yellow to white running across the blade. Occasionally pinkish flower plumes produced but grown chiefly for its banding. Tends to come up green and then the bands develop throughout the season.

Miscanthus sinensis 'Zebrinus' Zebra Grass (grass)
Height: Europe and USA 8ft (2.4m).
Spread: 4ft (1.2m).
Hardiness: Europe Zone 6; USA Zone 5. Deciduous.

Similar in its markings to 'Strictus' but of a more lax habit and not as full. Older than 'Strictus', being introduced in 1877. Occasionally produces flower plumes but mainly grown for its foliage.

Miscanthus Yakushima dwarf. This group has now been divided into clear forms, 'Abundance' and 'Elfin' being two.

Miscanthus sinensis 'Abundance'
Height: Europe and USA 5ft (1.5m).
Spread: 3ft 3in (1m).
Hardiness: Europe Zone 5; USA Zone 6. Sun or part shade; deciduous.

Previously one of the grasses in the Yakushima dwarf group. This cultivar was named by Knoll Gardens to

identify it from others in the previous group. Narrow delicate leaves in a dense mound with buff white flowers.

Miscanthus sinensis 'Adagio'
Height: Europe 5ft to 6ft 6in (1.5m to 2m); USA 5ft (1.5m).
Spread: 3ft 3 in (1m).
Hardiness: Europe Zone 5; USA Zone 6. Sunny open site; deciduous.

Slender leaves and many erect pale flower plumes in August, red turning to white with age. Bred by Kurt Bluemel.

Miscanthus sinensis 'Afrika'
Height: Europe and USA 5ft (1.5m).
Spread: 4ft (1.2m).
Hardiness: Europe Zone 5; USA Zone 6. Sunny open site; deciduous.

A good variety for autumn foliage, which turns an orange-scarlet colour much earlier than other Miscanthus varieties.

Miscanthus sinensis 'Andante'
Height: Europe and USA 6ft 6 in (2m).
Spread: 4ft (1.2m).
Hardiness: Europe Zone 5; USA Zone 6. Sunny open site; deciduous.

Pink flower plumes showing above tight mounds of green foliage. Another Kurt Bluemel selection.

Miscanthus sinensis 'Autumn Light'
Height: Europe 6ft to 7ft (1.8m to 2.1m); USA 8ft (2.4m).
Spread: 5ft (1.5m).
Hardiness: Europe Zone 5; USA Zone 6. Sunny site; deciduous.

Narrow green foliage turning yellow to red in autumn. Tall flower plumes beige in summer. Delicate arching foliage.

Miscanthus sinensis 'Blutenwunder'
Height: Europe and USA 5ft (1.5m).
Spread: 4ft (1.2m).
Hardiness: Europe Zone 7; USA Zone 6. Sunny open site; deciduous.

Bluish green leaves in abundance and a very good bloomer.

Miscanthus sinensis 'China'
Height: Europe and USA 5ft (1.5m).
Spread: 4ft (1.2 m).
Hardiness: Europe Zone 7; USA Zone 6.
Sunny site; deciduous.

Dark green foliage that may flush reddish after a hot summer. Large red flower plumes fading to whitish brown with age. Good autumn colour.

Miscanthus sinensis 'Dixieland'
Height: Europe and USA 6ft (1.8m).
Spread: 4ft (1.2 m).
Hardiness: Europe Zone 7; USA Zone 6.
Sun or part shade; deciduous.

Arching leaves with margins and longitudinal lines of a pale yellow colour that age to creamy white.

Miscanthus sinensis 'Elfin'
Height: Europe and USA 5ft (1.5m).
Spread: 3ft 3 in (1m).
Hardiness: Europe Zone 7; USA Zone 6.
Sun or part shade; deciduous.

Another of the cultivars from the group previously known as Yakushima dwarf. Mounds of narrow leaves with masses of light pinky-white flower plumes on a red stem. Named by Knoll Gardens.

Miscanthus sinensis 'Emmanuel Lepage'
Height: Europe and USA 6ft 6 in (2m).
Spread: 5ft (1.5m).
Hardiness: Europe Zone 7; USA Zone 6.
Sunny site; deciduous.

Wide arching leaves with dark pink flower plumes, very fluffy and ageing whitish.

Miscanthus sinensis 'Ghana'
Height: Europe and USA 6ft (1.8m).
Spread: 5ft (1.5m).
Hardiness: Europe Zone 7; USA Zone 6.
Sunny site; deciduous.

Dense erect clumps of foliage. Slender reddish brown flower plumes. Autumn foliage reddish orange. A selection by Pagels.

Miscanthus sinensis 'Goliath'
Height: Europe and USA to 9ft (2.7m).
Spread: 5ft (1.5m).
Hardiness: Zone 4.
Sunny site; deciduous.

Another of the larger specimens. Brownish red flower plumes ageing pinky silver. Good upright habit.

Miscanthus sinensis 'Hermann Mussel'
Height: Europe and USA to 6ft 6in (2m).
Spread: 5ft (1.5m).
Hardiness: Zone 4.
Sunny site; deciduous.

Wide leaves with prominent white midrib. Pinky brown flower plumes which turn silvery with age and close up in their habit. An introduction from Pagels.

Miscanthus sinensis 'Malepartus'
Height: Europe and USA 2.1m (7ft).
Spread: 1.2m (4ft).
Hardiness: Europe Zone 7; USA Zone 5.
Deciduous.

Miscanthus sinensis 'Morning Light'
Height: Europe 5ft (1.5m); USA 6ft 6in (2 m).
Spread: 4ft (1.2m).
Hardiness: Zone 5.
Sunny site; deciduous.

Perhaps one of the most useful and graceful *Miscanthus* available to gardeners. Narrow leaves with white borders that can look silver from a distance. An upright habit that gracefully arches towards the top. Not noted for producing flower plumes but if it does, they are pinkish in colour. A well-established plant first introduced into the United States in 1976 and named by Kurt Bluemel.

Miscanthus sinensis 'Nippon'
Height: Europe and USA 5ft (1.5m).
Spread: 3ft (90cm).
Hardiness: Europe Zone 5; USA Zone 6.
Sunny site; deciduous.

Compact form with slender flower plumes, early flowering and red in colour. The foliage has a coppery tinge in autumn.

Miscanthus sinensis 'Professor Richard Hansen'
Height: Europe and USA 8ft (2.4m).
Spread: 5ft (1.5m).
Hardiness: Europe Zone 4; USA Zone 5.
Sunny site; deciduous.

Broad green foliage with tall upright flower plumes, red to begin with, fading to beige-white, becoming more fluffy with age.

Miscanthus sinensis 'Roland'
Height: Europe and USA 8ft (2.4m).
Spread: 7ft (2.1m).
Hardiness: Zone 7.
Sunny site; deciduous.

A tall specimen with pinkish white flower plumes held well above the foliage.

Miscanthus sinensis 'Sarabande'
Height: Europe and USA to 6ft 6in (2m).
Spread: 3ft 3in (1m).
Hardiness: Zone 5.
Sunny site; deciduous.

Fine narrow foliage topped by a golden-brown flower plume in late summer. Introduced by Kurt Bluemel's nursery.

Miscanthus 'Undine', seen here at RHS Garden Harlow Carr, North Yorkshire, a part of a herbaceous planting with *Aconitum*.

Miscanthus 'Silberfeder' was bred in Germany, hence the translation of Silver Feather.

Miscanthus sinensis 'Silberfeder'
Height: Europe and USA to 7ft (2.1m).
Spread: 4ft (1.2m).
Hardiness: Europe Zone 5; USA Zone 4.
Sunny site; deciduous.

This form has been around since the 1970s but is still very garden-worthy. The flower plumes are reddish pink in late summer, ageing to silver. Foliage deep green tinted yellow in autumn.

Miscanthus sinensis 'Undine'
Height: Europe and USA 7ft (2.1m).
Spread: 3ft 3in (1m).
Hardiness: Zone 7.
Sunny site; deciduous.

Russet pink flower plumes fading to silvery white and becoming fluffy late in the season. Slender foliage that turns yellow in autumn.

Miscanthus sinensis 'Zwergelefant'
Height: Europe and USA 7ft (2.1m).
Spread: 5ft (1.5m).
Hardiness: Zone 7.
Sunny site; deciduous.

The most outstanding feature of this variety is the crinkled pinkish flower plumes that emerge from a trunk-like shape (hence its name 'Little Elephant'). Coarse broad leaves.

Miscanthus transmorrisonensis Taiwanese Miscanthus
Height: Europe 4ft (1.2m); USA 3ft 3 in (1m).
Spread: 3ft 3in (1m).
Hardiness: Europe Zone 7; USA Zone 6.
Sun or part shade; deciduous.

Dependent on location in the world, the foliage will be retained for long periods, well into December in the UK and fully evergreen in Southern California. Narrow glossy foliage with pinkish flower plumes fading to golden-white. Originally from medium to high altitudes in Taiwan. Comes true from seed.

Miscanthus transmorrisoniensis. Taiwanese Miscanthus is a fine form from Taiwan.

A tall, graceful grass. Large mounds of bright green foliage support airy stems of purplish to straw-coloured flowers. The whole plant turns golden yellow in autumn.

Molinia caerulea **'Transparent'**
As above but slightly smaller in Europe at 6ft (1.8m).

Muhlenbergia rigens Deer Grass (grass)
Height: Europe 4ft (1.2m); USA 5ft (1.5m).
Spread: 3ft 3in (1m).
Hardiness: Europe Zone 9; USA Zone 7.
Evergreen.

Large clumps formed of grey-green leaves from which emerge silvery grey flower spikes that turn buff in winter but are retained. As it is draught tolerant, it makes a good containerized specimen plant.

Molinia caerulea subsp. *Arundinacea* **'Skyracer'**
Tall Purple Moor Grass (grass)
Height: Europe and USA 8ft (2.4m).
Spread: 4ft (1.2m).
Hardiness: Europe Zone 5; USA Zone 4.
Sunny site; deciduous.

Panicum virgatum **'Blue Tower'** Switch Grass, Panic Grass (grass)
Height: Europe 8ft (2.4m); USA 9ft (2.7m).
Spread: 3ft 3in (1m).
Hardiness: Europe Zone 5; USA Zone 4.
Deciduous.

Probably the bluest of the Panicums. Tall, upright, glaucous blue foliage with long flower plumes. Needs good drainage.

Panicum virgatum **'Cloud Nine'** Switch Grass (grass)
Height: Europe and USA 8ft (2.4m).
Spread: 5ft (1.5m).
Hardiness: Europe Zone 5; USA Zone 4.
Deciduous.

Tall, upright variety, staying so throughout the winter in its dead foliage form. Good blue colour with the bonus of a lively autumn colour of dark gold. As with the other blue Panicums, requires good drainage to perform well.

Panicum virgatum **'Dallas Blue'** Switch Grass (grass)
Height: Europe and USA 5ft (1.5m).
Spread: 3ft 3in (1m).
Hardiness: Europe Zone 5; USA Zone 4.
Deciduous.

Molinia 'Skyracer' (tall Purple moor grass), an aptly-named thin, very upright grass forming an elegant shape against the skyline.

A relatively new introduction. Glaucous blue colour with wide leaves. Upright habit which slightly turns at the top. Good mauve coloured seed heads and yellow autumn foliage colour.

Panicum virgatum 'Heavy metal' (Blue switch grass), seen here combined in a suitable herbaceous combination at The Walled Garden, Scampston, North Yorkshire.

Panicum virgatum 'Heavy Metal' Blue Switch Grass (grass)
Height: Europe 3ft 3 in (1m); USA 5ft (1.5m).
Spread: 3ft (90cm).
Hardiness: Europe Zone 5; USA Zone 4.
Deciduous.

One of the first blue Panicums. It has thinner leaf blades but a good upright habit. Flower heads are purplish brown. Not as intensely blue as the newer cultivars and produces a better colour in USA but still worthy of a place in the garden. In the early autumn, the leaves develop a purple hue and then golden.

Panicum virgatum 'Warrior' Switch Grass (grass)
Height: Europe and USA 5ft (1.5m).
Spread: 4ft (1.2m).
Hardiness: Europe Zone 5; USA Zone 4.
Deciduous.

An upright habit with green foliage that has elements of a deep red/purple. Good golden autumn colour and a profusion of small purple flowers.

Sorghastrum nutans Indian Grass (grass)
Height: Europe 5ft (1.5m); USA 5ft to 8ft depending on range (1.5m to 2.4m).
Spread: 3ft 3in (1m).
Hardiness: Zone 4.
Deciduous.

A native grass of America that was a constituent part of the tall grass prairie. In the UK, the leaf colour tends to be green/grey but given more heat in parts of Europe and the USA, it can develop a blue colour. An attractive feature is the bright yellow pollen sacs that are produced from the flower heads in late summer. Autumn colour is a bright yellow fading to a light brown and the dead foliage is retained upright throughout the winter.

Stipa extremiorientalis Needle Grass, Feather Grass (grass)
Height: Europe and USA 4ft (1.2m).
Spread: 3ft 3in (1m).
Hardiness: Zone 6.
Deciduous.

Erect wide leaves of a yellowy green colour. Panicles produced late summer and green in colour. The foliage colour in winter starts yellow then fades to beige, which contrasts well with the panicles, which turn black.

Stipa gigantea Spanish Oat Grass, Golden Oats (grass)
Height: Europe 6ft (1.8m); USA 8ft (2.4m).
Spread: 6ft (1.8m).
Hardiness: Europe Zone 8; USA Zone 6.
Evergreen.

A spectacular feature plant or, if the room is available, for large drift planting. Fine dark green basal growth up to about 75cm from which are produced oat-like seed heads of golden colour that shimmer and sway in the breeze. The panicles then fade to a straw colour but are retained throughout most of the winter on the upright stems.

Stipa gigantea (Golden Oats), Even when the seed has dropped from the heads, the effect is wonderful.

Stipa gigantea 'Gold Fontaene'. A mass planting at RHS Garden Harlow Carr, North Yorkshire, providing a screen but still allowing views through to other parts of the garden.

BELOW: *Carex pendula* (Pendulous sedge). The strong foliage of pendula, a plant that will grow in most situations.

***Stipa gigantea* 'Gold Fontaene'** Oat Grass (grass)
Height: Europe 6ft (1.8m); USA 8ft (2.4m).
Spread: 6ft (1.8m).
Hardiness: Europe Zone 8; USA Zone 6.
Evergreen.

All the attributes of the parent plant but this selection has much larger flower heads.

Tall grasses for shade

Carex pendula Weeping or Pendulous Sedge (sedge)
Height: Europe 5ft (1.5m); USA 6ft 6in (2m).
Spread: 3ft 3in (1m).
Hardiness: Zone 8.
Evergreen.

A native to Europe. Dark green wide foliage forming a tight clump. Leaves pendulous towards the top. Produces many attractive pendulous seed heads held above the plant like short tails. Green to start with, these turn brown with age and then drop off. A very tough plant which can self seed very easily.

Deschampsia caespitosa 'Bronzeschleier (Tussock grass). The delicate seed heads held well clear of the basal clump dance in the wind with the slightest movement.

Carex pendula 'Moonraker' The new foliage shows a lovely yellow colour in spring.

Small clumps of green foliage produce a profusion of bronze flowers on stems about 1m high in late spring to early summer. These will remain throughout the winter months until they are broken down by the weather.

Carex pendula **'Moonraker'** Weeping or Pendulous Sedge (sedge)
Height: Europe 3ft 3in (1m); USA 5ft (1.5m).
Spread: 3ft 3in (1m).
Hardiness: Zone 8.
Evergreen.

A variegated sport of *pendula*. The new foliage is a striking mild butter-yellow colour that is retained for most of the season as the plant grows, but gradually turns green towards the end of summer. Very attractive and not quite as vigorous as *pendula*.

Tall grasses for part shade

Deschampsia caespitosa **'Bronzeschleier'**
Tussock Grass, Hair Grass (grass)
Height: Europe 3ft 3in (1m); USA 4ft (1.2m).
Spread: 2ft 6in (75cm).
Hardiness: Zone 4.
Deciduous.

Miscanthus sinensis var. **condensatus** **'Cosmopolitan'** (grass)
Height: Europe 7ft (2.4m); USA 10ft (3m).
Spread: 4ft (1.2m).
Hardiness: Europe Zone 7; USA Zone 6.
Deciduous.

The reverse colouring of 'Cabaret' being creamy white with a green centre, although the colours may not be as deep as 'Cabaret'. Similar in habit being upright. Flowers more frequently than Cabaret, coppery red flowers in late summer.

Miscanthus sinensis **'Dixieland'** (grass)
Height: Europe 4ft (1.2m); USA 5ft (1.5m).
Spread: 4ft (1.2m).
Hardiness: Europe Zone 7; USA Zone 6.
Deciduous.

A smaller variegated *Miscanthus* having pale yellow stripes that age cream on a fresh green leaf. Because of its height, it makes an excellent potted subject.

Miscanthus transmorrisoniensis (grass)
Height: Europe 5ft (1.5m); USA 3ft 3in
(1m).
Spread: 3ft 3in (1m).
Hardiness: Europe Zone 7; USA Zone 6.
Deciduous.

Dark narrow green leaves, almost evergreen
in Europe and evergreen in California. Flower
heads pinkish-white, held high over basal
foliage, turning golden yellow to brown.
Originally from medium to high altitudes in
Taiwan. Comes true from seed.

Stipa extremiorientalis Needle Grass,
Feather Grass (grass)
Height: Europe and USA 4ft (1.2m).
Spread: 3ft 3in (1m).
Hardiness: Europe Zone 6; USA Zone 6
Deciduous.

Erect wide leaves of a yellowy green colour. Panicles
produced late summer are green in colour. The
foliage colour in winter starts yellow then fades to
beige, which contrasts well with the panicles that
turn black.

Tall grasses for damp areas

Cyperus papyrus Egyptian Paper Reed (reed)
Height: Europe 12ft (3.6m); USA 15ft (4.5m).
Spread: 4ft (1.2m).
Hardiness: Zone 9.
Evergreen.

Majestic reed. Leafless stems topped with wide
inflorescences (30cm). Must never dry out so best
grown in water and given frost protection indoors. Can
be grown in a large pot stood in a tray of water.

Cyperus ustulatus (reed)
Height: Europe 5ft (1.5m); USA 6ft (1.8m).
Spread: 4ft (1.2m).
Hardiness: Europe Zone 8; USA Zone 7.
Evergreen.

Broad parchment-like leaves at the base. Airy flower
heads usually dark or yellow brown. Will grow as a
marginal in a pond or in garden soil that is moisture
retentive. Prefers a sunny open site. Originated from
New Zealand.

Equisetum hyemale (horsetail). A marvellously architectural
plant with tall upright stems that combines well in urban
domestic plantings with modern buildings.

Equisetum hyemale Horsetail (Equisetaceae)
Height: Europe and USA 5ft (1.5m).
Spread: Will continue until checked.
Hardiness: Zone 6.
Semi-evergreen.

Hollow upright stems, bright green when young,
turning darker with age. Dark brown nodes, which
give it a horizontal-banded look for the full length of
each stem, tapering towards the tip. Prefers moist to
wet conditions and a sunny site. Advisable to grow in
pots or contained in some way as it has the ability to
spread through the ground. Usually evergreen, except
in harsh winters, but it is probably best to cut all old
foliage away in spring and allow fresh growth to come
through.

Miscanthus sacchariflorus
Height: Europe 10ft (3m); USA 8ft (2.4m).
Spread: Will continue until checked.
Hardiness: Europe Zone 7; USA Zone 7.
Deciduous.

A very large *Miscanthus* that is useful for making a bold
foliage statement. Bamboo-like stems with wide bright
green leaves. Spreads slowly and is not invasive but will
require a large space to grow into. Rarely flowers in
the UK.

Phragmites australis variegatus Common Reed
(reed)
Height: Europe 7ft (2.4m); USA 8ft (2.4m).
Spread: Will continue until checked.
Hardiness: Europe Zone 5; USA Zone 3.
Deciduous.

Yellow striped leaves that age white, with purplish
red flower heads on tall stems. Sunny or partly
shaded site is preferred and it must have sufficient
moisture. Best grown in a pot or contained in a
large bed as it has the ability to spread rapidly in
damp ground.

Schoenoplectus albescens White Bulrush, Candy
Rush (sedge)
Height: Europe and USA 5ft (1.5m).
Spread: 5ft (1.5m).
Hardiness: Europe Zone 4; USA Zone 5.
Deciduous.

Upright stems almost white but actually striped
vertically light green and white. Clusters of
brownish flowers on the higher portion of the
plant. Sunny site preferred. Must have moisture to
thrive, in any amount from marginal planting to very
damp ground.

Typha angustifolia Narrow Leaved Bulrush or Reed
Mace (reed)
Height: Europe 5ft (1.5m); USA 6ft 6in (2m).
Spread: Will continue until checked.
Hardiness: Zone 3.
Deciduous.

Native plant to Europe, the Americas and Asia. Dark
green leaves. Dark to reddish brown female spikes.
Must have water or very wet ground. Sunny open site.

***Typha latifolia* 'Variegata'** Cat-tail (reed)
Height: Europe 4ft (1.2m); USA 10ft (3m).
Spread: Will continue until checked.
Hardiness: Europe Zone 4; USA Zone 3.
Deciduous.

Variegated form of common bulrush. Creamy white
and green variegated foliage. Much less vigorous
than the typical form. Distinctive female seed head
which is dark reddish brown. Must have moisture in
the ground or as an aquatic marginal. Makes a good
containerized specimen.

MEDIUM GRASSES

A selection of grasses that, at maturity, will be
approximately 60cm to 1.2m tall.

Medium grasses for a hot site

Achnatherum calamagrostis Silver Needle Grass
(grass)
Height: Europe 3ft (90cm); USA 3ft 3in (1m).
Spread: 3ft 3in (1m).
Hardiness: Zone 5.
Deciduous.

Previously classified as a Stipa, this grass puts on a
wonderful show of densely tufted seed heads turning a
buff colour from silver. These are produced on top of a
clump of refined medium green foliage. Prefers a sunny
site and a free-draining soil.

Ammophila arenaria Marram Grass (grass)
Height: Europe to 3ft 3in (1m); USA 1ft to 3ft 3in
(30cm to 1m).
Spread: Will continue until checked.
Hardiness: Zone 5.
Semi-evergreen.

A native of Europe and North Africa, Marram is used
to stabilize sand dunes, which gives some idea of its
invasive capacity. Indeed, this led to the displacement of
some native dune species when it was used in the west
coast of America and is now considered an invasive
exotic. Tough grey-green foliage with strong upright
buff flower heads. The nearer the soil conditions to
sand, the better it does.

Anementhele lessoniana Pheasant's Tail Grass (grass)
Height: Europe and USA 3ft 3in (1m).
Spread: 3ft 3in (1m).
Hardiness: Europe Zone 8; USA Zone 7.
Evergreen.

Anementhele × lessoniana (Pheasant tail grass). With green
foliage turning yellow, red and orange with autumn and a
very fine seed head, this is a very attractive grass.

One of the most useful grasses for the garden, tolerating a wide range of situations. Forms graceful mounds of foliage mostly green in colour but as autumn approaches, tans, oranges and reds appear. Very delicate seed heads, pink in colour, are produced on lax thin stems that give the impression of a pink cloud around the grass. It grows well in sunny sites but is quite happy in shade, although does not produce the colours as well as when in an open site. Prefers a free-draining soil and doesn't do well in wet conditions or when it is divided up. Fortunately, the plant comes easily from seed and may self-seed in the garden but not to nuisance levels. Originates from New Zealand.

Briza media Quaking Grass, Tottergrass, Jiggle-joggles, Rattle Grass (grass)
Height: Europe 2ft (60cm); USA 3ft (90cm).
Spread: 2ft (60cm).
Hardiness: Europe Zone 5; USA Zone 4.
Semi-evergreen.

The wide range of common names indicates a familiarity with this native grass for many years. From a tight mound of green foliage, many delicate heads are sent up to about 2ft (60cm). As they dry, they become golden in colour and dance in the slightest breeze. From their emergence in May, they will be retained throughout the summer. Prefers a free-draining soil and sunny site but will tolerate some shade and a clayish soil.

Briza media 'Golden Bee'. Seen here on Knoll Gardens Gold Medal Awarded display (Chelsea 2011). An excellent form that retains its seed heads well into the late summer.

Briza media 'Golden Bee'

A selected form of the above, perhaps with a larger seed head and more golden colour.

Briza media 'Russell's'

A variegated form of Briza media, having white and green striped foliage.

Calamagrostis brachytricha (Korean feather grass). A grass with lovely delicate seed heads and a very upright habit. Seen here at RHS Garden, Wisley.

Calamagrostis brachytricha Korean Feather Reed Grass (grass)
Height: Europe and USA 4ft (1.2m).
Spread: 3ft 3in (1m).
Hardiness: Zone 4.
Deciduous.

Its greyish green leaves that turn orange or yellow in winter are very attractive but the seed head is stunning. Held upright above the plant, it is arrow shaped and made up of many small flowers, initially purplish grey in colour but opening to a pinky beige. It retains its upright position throughout the summer if planted in a soil with some moisture, more lax if planted in drier conditions. Prefers sunny site but will perform in part shade.

Calamagrostis varia Reed Grass (grass)
Height: Europe 3ft to 4ft (90cm to 1.2m); USA 4ft (1.2 m).
Spread: 3ft 3in (1m).
Hardiness: Zone 5.
Deciduous.

Very attractive deep reddish purple flowers held on upright stems. Dense clump-forming grass with a slender leaf. Native of central and southern Europe. Prefers a sunny site in the garden but can tolerate the light shade in which it grows in the wild as well as on mountain grassland, often on calcareous soils.

Carex pendula Pendulous Sedge (sedge)
Height: Europe 3ft (90cm) USA 3ft 3in (1m).
Spread: 3ft 3in (1m).
Hardiness: Europe Zone 8; USA Zone 8.
Evergreen.

A native to the UK and West and Central Europe and North Africa, pendula is often criticized for its ability to self-seed and survive, if not thrive, in most conditions, but placed in the right context, it can fill a number of requirements. Dense clumps of wide green foliage from a basal clump of about 60cm from which a tall stem emerges with a dropping yellow catkin-type flower. Will grow successfully in sun or shade and both wet and dry soils, and often thrives quite happily in the cracks between paving and buildings in courtyards.

Carex pendula 'Moonraker'
With all the attributes of the above although not quite as vigorous. In spring, all the new foliage is a wonderful yellow colour that turns green as the season progresses.

Carex tenuiculmis Brown Sedge (sedge)
Height: Europe and USA 2ft (60cm).
Spread: 3ft 3in (1m).
Hardiness: Zone 6.
Evergreen.

Attractive habit arching gently at the top and so not lying on the ground. Chocolate coloured foliage containing a range of reds and browns. Happy in sun or part shade. Originated in New Zealand.

Carex tenuiculmis (brown sedge). A gracefully dropping form that shows itself off best in a raised container.

Carex testacea Orange Sedge (sedge)
Height: Europe and USA 18in (45cm).
Spread: 18in (45cm).
Hardiness: Europe Zone 7; USA Zone 6.
Evergreen.

A very attractive and neat plant arching gracefully towards its top. The foliage is green at the base, changing to a pleasant strong orange colour at the top of the plant. This orange colour intensifies throughout the season, especially when it is planted in a sunny position. A very good plant for containers as it is not too large and display of its arching habit is more pronounced when it is clear of the ground. Round seed heads borne on dropping stems that touch the ground. Another native sedge of New Zealand.
'Old Gold' is a selected form that has more golden colouration, although not to such a degree that it is vastly different.

Chasmanthium latifolium Wild Oat Spangle Grass (grass)
Height: Europe 2ft (60cm); USA 4ft (1.2m).
Spread: 1ft (30cm).
Hardiness: Europe Zone 6; USA Zone 5.
Deciduous.

A clump-forming grass from the USA. Attractive green foliage turning gold in autumn. The seed head is the star of the plant, being flattened spikelets slightly resembling a goldfish. Green when they first appear, they then turn reddish bronze in the autumn and then a light buff colour and are splendid when viewed with the sun shining through them. In England the plant requires full sun, but in the USA it will grow happily in part shade, although the stems are more lax in those conditions.

Chionochloa rubra Red Tussock Grass (grass)
Height: Europe and USA 3ft 3in (1m).
Spread: 3ft 3in (1m).
Hardiness: Europe Zone 7; USA Zone 8.
Evergreen.

Dense clumps of copper-brown foliage (sometimes redder), which gently arches over. A native of New Zealand. Sunny position required and, once established, it is happy in very dry conditions.

Chondropetalum tectorum (restio)
Height: Europe 3ft 3in (1m); USA 4ft (1.2m).
Spread: 18in (45cm).
Hardiness: Europe Zone 8; USA Zone 8.
Evergreen.

Dark stems form an upright habit and radiate out and touch the ground where they grow nearer the base of the plant. Dark brown flowers at tips of foliage. Prefers a sunny position and a very well-drained soil, particularly in wet areas.

Deschampsia caespitosa Tufted Hair Grass (grass)
Height: Europe 2ft 6in (75cm); USA 4ft (1.2m).
Spread: 2ft 6in (75cm).
Hardiness: Zone 4.
Deciduous.

A native to the UK and the mountains of tropical Africa and Asia. Neat mounds of dark green foliage from which emerge a mass of billowing flower heads in several colours: silver, green, purple, turning straw

Deschampsia caespitosa (tufted hair grass), here grown against a background of *Panicum* 'Shenandoah' at The Walled Garden, Scampston, North Yorkshire.

yellow with age. These flower heads are retained over winter until broken down by the weather. Looks magnificent in a mass planting or where the seed heads can be seen against a dark background. Prefers some moisture in the ground and will thrive in a sunny or part shaded site.

Deschampsia caespitosa 'Bronzeschleier' A selected form of caespitosa with the same habit and size but bronze-coloured flowers on opening.
Deschampsia caespitosa 'Goldtau' A selected form with shorter flowering stems than caespitosa at 80–80cm.

Eragrostis curvula African Love Grass, Weeping Love Grass (grass)
Height: Europe 3ft (90cm); USA 3ft 3in (1m).
Spread: 4ft (1.2m).
Hardiness: Europe Zone 6; USA Zone 7.
Deciduous.

Although native to Africa, this grass has proved surprisingly hardy in other areas. It forms a wide tussock of fine grass, which supports, in a lax habit, a great profusion of fine stems with very fine seed heads. Green on emerging, the seed heads turn tan or beige with age. Useful as a garden plant, and in southern USA it is also used as a plant to stabilize embankments and other areas of soil erosion. Always prefers a sunny situation and free-draining soil.

Eragrostis 'Totnes Burgundy' A selected form having grey flower plumes on opening. Mature leaves turn a deep burgundy colour. Introduced by Sarah and Julian Sutton of Totnes, Devon.

Eragrostis Elliottii (love grass). A large delicate mound is formed by this grass with arching seed heads.

Eragrostis elliottii Love Grass (grass)
Height: Europe 2ft 6in (75cm); USA 4ft (1.2m).
Spread: 3ft (90cm).
Hardiness: Europe Zone 8; USA Zone 7.
Deciduous.

A native species of North America. Thin blue grey leaves provide a mound of foliage to support the billowing seed heads. Sunny spot with very free-draining soil is required.

Eragrostis trichodes Sand Love Grass (grass)
Height: Europe 3ft (90cm); USA 4ft (1.2m).
Spread: 3ft (90cm).
Hardiness: Zone 5.
Deciduous.

A native of USA and, as its name suggests, this species likes sandy or free-draining soil. Deep green leaves and a profusion of reddish pink panicles. Sunny site required.

Festuca californica Californian Fescue (grass)
Height: Europe and USA 3ft (90cm).
Spread: 2ft to 3ft (60–90cm).
Hardiness: Europe Zone 8; USA Zone 7.
Semi-evergreen.

Blue-green or glaucous blue-grey foliage forms a loose mound. Flower heads green to bluish green, ageing to purple then straw yellow. Often stays dormant during dry periods, only then sending up new growth in the autumn. Sunny open site, or light shade in areas of high sunlight.

Festuca mairei Atlas Fescue (grass)
Height: Europe to 3ft 3in (1m); USA 2ft 6in (80cm).
Spread: 2ft (60cm).
Hardiness: Zone 5.
Evergreen.

Forming a distinct rounded outline of grey-green foliage with very slender panicles green in colour. Dislikes wet conditions, particularly in winter, so a sunny, free-draining site necessary. Native to the Atlas Mountains of Morocco.

Helictotrichon sempervirens Blue Oat Grass (grass)
Height: Europe and USA 2ft 6in (80cm).
Spread: 2ft 6in (80cm).
Hardiness: Zone 4.
Semi-evergreen.

A native of the Mediterranean region, this grass prefers a sunny, free-draining site, although in high sunlight areas it will accept light shade. In damp ground conditions, rust can be a problem. Silver-blue foliage forms an erect habit and is clump

Helictotrichon sempervirens (Blue oat grass). Originating from the Mediterranean, the steely blue colour of this grass makes it useful in both hot borders and containers.

forming. Flower plumes yellow or buff, although it does not flower as profusely as other grasses, especially if conditions are humid. Makes a splendid container plant.

Hordeum jubatum Foxtail Barley (grass)
Height: Europe 20in (50cm); USA 2ft 6in (80cm).
Spread: 1ft (30cm).
Hardiness: Europe Zone 5; USA Zone 4.
Deciduous.

A short-lived perennial grass for perhaps two years or so and therefore best treated as an annual in the UK. It does, however, reliably seed itself. Grown mainly for its showy flower heads, which resemble cultivated barley but are silver pink in appearance. Foliage is insignificant. Due to its self-seeding capabilities it has become a noxious weed in some countries, such as Western United States. In the UK, it has become naturalized but is not a problem.

Hystrix patula Bottle Brush Grass (grass)
Height: Europe and USA 1m (3ft 3in).
Spread: 2ft (60cm).
Hardiness: Zone 4.
Deciduous.

Coarse green foliage with an upright flower spike that resembles a bottle brush, although more spikey in appearance. Light or pinkish green in colour, ageing to brown. Sun or part shade.

Jarava ichu Peruvian Feather Grass (grass)
Height: Europe and USA 3ft (90cm).
Spread: 2ft 6in (80cm).
Hardiness: Zone 8.
Semi-evergreen.

Soft green foliage topped by long, narrow, fluffy white flowers that move gracefully with the slightest breeze. Must have a free-draining soil and a sunny site.

Leymus arenarius (Sea Lyme Grass). Happy on sandy ground, indeed it grows well on sand dunes.

Leymus arenarius Sea Lyme Grass (grass)
Height: Europe 3ft 3in (1m); USA 4ft (1.2m).
Spread: Will continue until checked.
Hardiness: Europe Zone 6; USA Zone 4.
Semi-evergreen.

A native of the UK, this plant grows on sandy shores and dunes and as such has a very invasive habit. Glaucous blue, flat leaves and a seed head reminiscent of wheat. Naturally prefers a sunny site with free-draining soil. Its toughness means it can be used on inhospitable sites such as traffic islands. Favourite grass of garden designer Gertrude Jekyll.

Melinis nerviglumis Pink Crystals, Ruby Grass (grass)
Height: Europe and USA 2ft (60cm).
Spread: 1ft (30cm).
Hardiness: Zone 9.
Evergreen in mild climates.

Blue-green foliage flushed purple in autumn. Spikelets ruby red to pink at first and then iridescent pink. Unlikely to be hardy in the UK, requiring frost-free protection.

Miscanthus 'Gold Bar'. A miniature version of *Miscanthus Zebrinus* for those who haven't the room in the garden for the large version.

***Miscanthus sinensis* 'Gold Bar'** (grass)
Height: Europe and USA 3ft (90cm).
Spread: 1ft (30cm).
Hardiness: Zone 6.
Deciduous.

A miniature version of the Zebra-striped Miscanthus. Gold barring appears on emergence of the foliage. Requires a sunny site.

'Little Zebrinus' is a smaller version of Zebrinus, only reaching 5ft (1.5m) in height and 1ft (30cm) wide. Wine-red flowers in late summer. Sunny site.

***Molinia caerulea* 'Edith Dudszus'** Purple Moor Grass (grass)
Height: Europe and USA 4ft (1.2m).
Spread: 3ft (90cm).
Hardiness: Zone 5.
Deciduous.

A neat basal clump of thin, bright green foliage. Thin flower stems, purple in colour, and dense flower spikes that are dark purple, almost black. Good autumn colour.
Sunny site.

'Moorhexe' is as above but only 2ft 6in (80cm) high. Good winter colour.

Nassella tenuissima (*Stipa tenuissima*). A grass that instantly brings movement to a border. Mass plantings sway gently in the breeze, seen here at RHS Garden Harlow Carr, North Yorkshire.

Nassella tenuissima Mexican Feather Grass, Pony Tails (grass)
Height: Europe and USA 2ft (60cm).
Spread: 2ft (60cm).
Hardiness: Europe Zone 7; USA Zone 6.
Evergreen.

Previously classified as a *Stipa* and probably one of the most-used grasses in the garden. Narrow mid-green foliage gives way to beige flower heads that move beautifully in the slightest breeze. A native of Texas, Mexico and Argentina, it therefore prefers a sunny site and a very free-draining soil. Self-seeds freely and has naturalized in California and the Pacific North West.

Oryzopsis millacea Indian Rice Grass, Smilo Grass (grass)
Height: Europe and USA 2ft (60cm).
Spread: 2ft (60cm).
Hardiness: Europe Zone 6; USA Zone 8. Semi-evergreen.

Evergreen clumps of deep green leaves that are deciduous in cold winters. Flower plumes arch upwards and outwards. It has the ability to self-seed, which has caused some problems in warmer areas. Sunny site.

Panicum virgatum Common Switch Grass (grass)
Height: Europe and USA 4ft to 8ft (1.2 to 2.4m).
Spread: 3ft (90cm).
Hardiness: Europe Zone 5; USA Zone 4. Deciduous.

The *Panicum virgatum* family of cultivars form a wide range of exceptionally good grasses for the garden. Originating from the American prairie, *Panicum virgatum* forms a clump but may be lax and billowing or erect and narrow in its growth habit. Both types will stand well into winter, perhaps bending with heavy rains but standing upright again once dry. The cultivars fall into two colour groups, one having glaucous blue foliage and the second green foliage. Both groups have good autumnal colour, although the blue group turns yellow and golden and not as red as the green group.

'Hanse Herme' grows to 4ft (1.2m) and has green foliage and a relaxed habit. Dark red colouring in late summer which turns to burgundy by autumn. Sunny site.

'Heavy Metal' grows to 5ft (1.5m), with strong glaucous blue colouring and a very upright habit. Stands well in winter weather. Inflorescences have pinkish purple tones.

'Shenandoah' Height 4ft (1.2m); this is one of the best Switch grasses for red colouring. It starts green in early summer and takes on a dark red tone by late summer, then completely wine coloured by autumn. Sunny site.

'Squaw' Height: 4ft (1.2m). Green leaved variety taking on autumnal tints with pinky red flowers in late summer. Sunny site.

Panicum virgatum 'Shenandoah'. Fantastic deep red colouring on this variety of Switch grass seen here at The Walled Garden, Scampston, North Yorkshire.

Pennisetum alopecuroides Fountain Grass (grass)
Height: Europe 18in to 2ft 6in (45–80cm); USA 2ft to 3ft (60–90cm).
Spread: 2ft (60cm).
Hardiness: Zone 6. Deciduous.

A whole range of cultivars have been developed, all having the basic characteristics of a mound of green foliage with fluffy bottlebrush-shaped flowers held above the plant on slightly arching stems. In colder areas, a sunny site with good drainage is required for successful growing.

'Hameln' Height: 3ft (90cm). One of the more reliable forms for colder areas. Creamy white flowers.

'Little Bunny' Height: 18in (45cm). Developed from 'Hameln', a truly miniature specimen of Pennisetum. Does not flower as freely in colder climates.

'Moudry' Height: 2ft 6in (75cm). Dark green leaves form a neat basal clump. In warmer climates a dark

Pennisetum alopecuroides 'Hameln'. A popular variety of fountain grass.

purple head is borne on a stiff stem, just clear of the foliage in a warm year. In colder climates, the flower heads may not emerge from the mound of broad leaves and in the UK, may not even flower in some years. In the USA and warmer areas it can self-seed and this has been a problem when grown next to lawns, where it has colonized the turf.

'Red Head' Height: 2ft 6in to 3ft 3in (75cm to 1m). A recently introduced cultivar. Flowers early in the year, the flowers being red fading through purple to beige.

Pennisetum orientale Oriental Fountain Grass (grass)
Height: Europe 3ft 3in to 5ft (1–1.5m); USA 3ft 3in to 6ft (1–1.8m).
Spread: 2ft (60cm).
Hardiness: Zone 6.
Deciduous.

A selection of cultivars taller than the alopecurus group but perhaps not as cold tolerant. Foliage greyish green in large clumps. Flower heads above foliage long and poker shaped.

'Karley Rose' Height: 4ft (1.2m). Deep rose-pink flower heads fading to pale brown or white. Darker leaves than most, with a long flowering period.

Pennisetum orientale 'Karley Rose' (fountain grass). Delicate pink flowerheads that cover the plant in warm dry areas.

'Tall Tails' Height: 5ft to 6ft (1.5m to 1.8 m). Very long, thin, semi-pendulous flower heads, white in colour, held on long stems.

Pennisetum massaicum Foxtail Grass (grass)
Represented by one cultivar in common garden use:
'Red Buttons'.
Height: Europe and USA 3ft (90cm).
Spread: 3ft (90cm).
Hardiness: Zone 8.
Deciduous.

Bright green foliage with a bright red, short, rounded
flower head that fades to tan and brown.

Phalaris arundinacea Reed Canary Grass (grass)
Height: Europe 2ft 6in to 3ft 3in (75 cm to 1m); USA
1.5m (5ft).
Spread: Will continue until checked.
Hardiness: Zone 4.
Deciduous.

A perennial species from North America and Eurasia.
Due to its ability to spread rapidly by rhizomes, it has
been used in the USA for forage and erosion control,
where it has invaded native wetlands and become a
nuisance. The cultivars used in the garden situation
are variegated and of European origin. However, they
have retained the spreading habit and so care has to be
taken in the siting and use of this grass. In the UK, the

early misuse of *Phalaris picta* (Gardener's gaiters) has
left a legacy of mistrust of all variegated grasses among
older amateur gardeners.

'Arctic Sun' Height: 2ft 6in (75cm). Relatively new
introduction having golden variegated foliage. Not as
vigorous as the species but still needs care in siting.
Foliage can be cut back mid-season to provide a fresh
flush for later in the year. Dampish to average soil in
sun or light shade.

'Feesey's Form' (also called **'Strawberries and
Cream'**) Height: 3ft (90cm). A much improved variety
of *Phalaris picta* with a clear white variegation running
down the green leaf. Foliage and stems can be tinted
pink in cool periods of spring and autumn. Foliage may
suffer in extreme heat. Selected by Mervyn Feesey of
Woodside Nursery, Devon.

Poa labillardierei Australian Blue Grass (grass)
Height: Europe and USA 4ft (1.2m).
Spread: 3ft 3in (1m).
Hardiness: Zone 8.
Deciduous.

Mounds of steely blue foliage with a succession of
silvery blue stems and flowers. Sun or part shade. In
cool climates prefers dry soil, but if grown in warmer
areas needs more moisture. Originating in south-east
Australia and Tasmania.

Schizachyrium scoparium Little Blue Stem (grass)
Height: Europe and USA 4ft (1.2m).
Spread: 2ft (60cm).
Hardiness: Europe Zone 4; USA Zone 3.
Deciduous.

Coming from the plains of North America, Little Blue
Stem is only little in comparison to Big Blue Stem.
Some selections have been made as forage plants but
are still attractive as garden specimens.

'Prairie Blues' Height: 3ft (90cm). Upright habit of
silvery grey-green foliage with seed heads at terminal
points of plant. In autumn leaves take on orange brown
hues. Full sun and a free-draining soil preferred but not
too rich in nutrients.

Phalaris arundinacea 'Feesey's' (Reed Canary Grass). A really
fast growing grass that needs a lot of room. Cut back mid-
season. It comes again for a bright show to finish off the year.

Spartina pectinata 'Aureomarginata'. A much underused graceful grass that does need a lot of room.

Spartina pectinata 'Aureomarginata' (grass)
Height: Europe and USA 7ft (2.1m).
Spread: Will continue until confined.
Hardiness: Europe Zone 3; USA Zone 4.
Deciduous.

This cultivar is the only one used in gardens. The species is Prairie Cord Grass, growing to a height of 7ft (2.1m) and happy in most soils, although would prefer some moisture in the soil. 'Aureomarginata' is a variegated version with bold yellow and green striped foliage, not as vigorous as the species but still spreading quite strongly.

Stipa tenuissima Mexican Feather Grass, Pony Tails (grass)
Height: Europe and USA 2ft (60cm).
Spread: 2ft (60cm).
Hardiness: Europe Zone 7; USA Zone 6.
Evergreen.

Now classified as *Nassella* and probably one of the most used grasses in the garden. Narrow mid green foliage gives way to beige flowerheads that move beautifully in the slightest breeze. Prefers a sunny site and a very free-draining soil due to its native home of Texas, Mexico and Argentina. Self-seeds freely and has naturalized in California and the Pacific North West.

Stipa barbata Feather Grass (grass)
Height: Europe and USA 2ft 6in (75cm).
Spread: 18in (45cm).
Hardiness: Europe Zone 7; USA Zone 8.
Deciduous.

The uninteresting foliage, green in colour, provides the base for stems with long arching awns (flower heads) 8in (19cm) long that move at the slightest breeze. Prefers a sunny site in free-draining soil.

Stipa calamagrostis Silver Spear Grass (grass)
See *Achnatherum calamagrostis* earlier in this section.

Medium grasses for part shade
Anementhele lessoniana Pheasant's Tail Grass (grass)
Height: Europe 3ft 3 in (1m); USA 3ft 3in (1m).
Spread: 3ft 3in (1m).
Hardiness: Europe Zone 8; USA Zone 7.
Evergreen.

One of the most useful grasses for the garden tolerating a wide range of situations. Forms graceful mounds of foliage mostly green in colour but as autumn approaches, tans, oranges and reds appear. Very delicate seed heads, pink in colour, are produced that are held on lax thin stems which gives the impression of a pink cloud around the grass. It grows well in sunny sites but is quite happy in shade, although does not produce the colours as well as when in an open site. Prefers a free draining soil and doesn't do well in wet conditions or when it is divided up. Fortunately, the plant comes easily from seed and may self-seed in the garden but not to nuisance levels. Originates from New Zealand.

Anementhele lessoniana 'Gold Hue' (grass)
Height: Europe 2ft to 2ft 6in (60 to 80cm); USA 3ft 3in (1m).
Spread: 3ft 3in (1m).
Hardiness: Europe Zone 8; USA Zone 7. Evergreen.

A selected form of the ever popular Pheasant's Tail Grass. Seldom seen in nursery catalogues but available from Knoll Gardens. Light yellowy-gold foliage for a longer period during autumn. Selected form by Graham Hutchins.

Briza 'Golden Bee' (Quaking grass). Seen here before the seeds turn golden brown, a delicate looking grass.

Briza media Quaking grass, Tottergrass, Jiggle-joggles, Rattle Grass (grass)
Height: Europe 2ft (60cm); USA 2ft 6 in (80cm).
Spread: 2ft (60cm).
Hardiness: Europe Zone 5; USA Zone 4. Semi evergreen.

The wide range of common names indicates the familiarity with this native grass for many years. From a

tight mound of green foliage, many delicate heads are sent up to about 2ft (60cm). As they dry, they become golden in colour and dance in the slightest breeze. From their emergence in May, they will be retained throughout the summer. Prefers a free draining soil and sunny site but will tolerate some shade and a clayish soil.

Briza media 'Golden Bee'
A selected form of the above, perhaps with a larger seed head and more golden colour.

Briza media 'Russells'
A variegated form of *Briza media*, having white and green striped foliage.

Carex elata aurea (Bowles Golden Sedge). A very garden-worthy sedge seen here just putting up new foliage after being cut back.

Carex elata 'Aurea' Bowles Golden Sedge (sedge)
Height: Europe and USA 2ft 6in (75cm).
Spread: 3ft (90cm).
Hardiness: Europe Zone 7; USA Zone 5. Semi-evergreen.

One of the best sedges for part shade, its brilliant colour lifting a shady spot. A graceful plant with deep golden-yellow leaves. The colour is better when in sun but still noteworthy, if not a little greener, in shade. Green stripe to edge of leaf. Growing from a tussock base, the leaves grow upright and then cascade down towards the ground. One of the older ornamental grasses, being found as a sport on Wicken Fen, Cambridgeshire, by E. A. Bowles in 1885.

Carex obnupta Slough Sedge (sedge)
Height: Europe 3ft to 4ft (90cm to 1.2m); USA 4ft (1.2 m).
Spread: Will continue until contained.
Hardiness: Zone 7.
Evergreen.

Large clumps of broadish green leaves with an attractive flower in midsummer, purplish black in colour. Will thrive in a moist to wet soil and can spread quickly in those conditions, being more restrained in a drier soil. A native of coastal California to British Columbia.

Carex pendula Pendulous Sedge (sedge)
Height: Europe 3ft (90cm); USA 3ft 3in (1m).
Spread: 3ft 3in (1m).
Hardiness: Europe Zone 8; USA Zone 8.
Evergreen.

A native to the UK and West and Central Europe and North Africa, pendula is often criticized for its ability to self-seed and survive, if not thrive, in most conditions, but placed in the right context, it can fill a number of requirements. Dense clumps of wide green foliage from a basal clump of about 2ft (60cm) from which a tall stem emerges with a dropping yellow catkin-type flower. Will grow successfully in sun or shade and both wet and dry soils, and often thrives quite happily in the cracks between paving and buildings in courtyards.

Carex pendula 'Moonraker'
This has all the attributes of the above, although not quite as vigorous. In spring, all the new foliage is a wonderful yellow colour that turns green as the season progresses.

Carex secta New Zealand Tussock Sedge (sedge)
Height: Europe and USA 4ft (1.2m).
Spread: 3ft 3in (1m).
Hardiness: Zone 8.
Evergreen.

Bright green leaves forming an arched shape, pale brown flower spikes in summer. Stems and root bases can form a 'trunk' in time. Prefers damp sites in the sun but will cope with part shade as long as moisture is present.

Carex trifida New Zealand Blue Sedge (sedge)
Height: Europe 3ft (90cm); USA 3ft 3in (1m).
Spread: 3ft 3in (1m).
Hardiness: Zone 7.
Evergreen.

Large keeled leaves, blue on the underside. Large reddish-brown flower heads borne early in the season. Dampish soil preferred but will tolerate a period of drought.

Chasmanthium latifolium Wild Oat Spangle Grass (grass)
Height: Europe 2 ft (60cm); USA 4ft (1.2m).
Spread: 1ft (30cm).
Hardiness: Europe Zone 6; USA Zone 5.
Deciduous.

A clump-forming grass from the USA. Attractive green foliage turning gold in autumn, The seed head is the star of the plant, being flattened spikelets slightly resembling a goldfish. Green when they first appear, they then turn reddish bronze in the autumn and then a light buff colour. Splendid when viewed with the sun shining through them. In England, the plant requires full sun, but in the USA it will grow happily in part shade although the stems are more lax in those conditions.

Deschampsia caespitosa Tufted Hair Grass (grass)
Height: Europe 2ft 6in (75cm); USA 4ft (1.2m).
Spread: 2ft 6in (75cm).
Hardiness: Europe Zone 4; USA Zone 4.
Deciduous.

A native to UK, mountains of tropical Africa and Asia. Neat mounds of dark green foliage from which emerge a mass of billowing flower heads in several colours, silver, green, purple turning straw yellow with age. These flowerheads are retained over winter until broken down by the weather. Looks magnificent in a mass planting or where the seed heads can be seen against a dark background. Prefers some moisture in the ground and will thrive in a sunny or part shaded site.

Deschampsia caespitosa 'Bronzeschleier' A selected form of caespitosa with the same habit and size but bronze coloured flowers on opening.

Deschampsia caespitosa 'Goldtau'
Height: Europe 2ft 6in (75cm); USA 3ft (90cm).
Spread: 2ft 6in (75cm).
Hardiness: Europe Zone 4; USA Zone 4.
Deciduous.

Neat clumps of green foliage that age golden brown. Short stems bear seeds, which are silver brown aging to a warm gold, and which stay on the plant all season in profusion.

Hystrix patula Bottle Brush Grass (grass)
Height: Europe 3ft 3in (1m); USA 3ft 3in (1m).
Spread: 2ft (60cm).
Hardiness: Europe Zone 4; USA Zone 4.
Deciduous.

Coarse green foliage with an upright flower spike that resembles a bottle brush, although more spiky in appearance. Light or pinkish green, ageing to brown in colour. Sun or part shade.

Miscanthus purpurascens Autumn Flame Miscanthus (grass)
Height: Europe 4ft (1.2m); USA 5ft (1.5m).
Spread: 4ft (1.2m).
Hardiness: Zone 4.
Deciduous.

One of the best *Miscanthus* for autumn colour, particularly in the USA. Leaves tinged reddish purple by the autumn then develop into brilliant red-orange. Shy to flower in Europe but in warm climates the flowers are pinkish, ageing to white. Sun or part shade. Autumnal colours may be more pastel in shade.

Miscanthus sinensis 'Little Kitten' (grass)
Height: Europe and USA 3ft 3in (1m).
Spread: 1ft (30cm).
Hardiness: Europe Zone 5; USA Zone 6.
Deciduous.

One of the smaller cultivars of *Miscanthus sinensis*. Mound-forming slender leaves with reddish flower heads, ageing brown to dull white. Sun or light shade preferred.

Miscanthus tinctoria 'Nanus Variegatus' (grass)
Height: Europe and USA 2ft 6in (75cm).
Spread: Will continue until contained.
Hardiness: Zone 7.
Deciduous.

Loose clumps of broad green leaves striped cream. Flowers pale brown but infrequent.

Molinia caerulea 'Poul Petersen' (purple moor grass). A neat clump forming plant used to great effect as a mass planting at The Walled Garden, Scampston, North Yorkshire.

Molinia caerulea 'Poul Petersen' Purple moor grass (grass)
Height: Europe and USA 3ft (90cm).
Spread: 3ft (90cm).
Hardiness: Zone 4.
Deciduous.

Upright form of bright green leaves, with purple flowers being held above the foliage. Both stems and leaves fade to a golden colour with the onset of autumn but retain their form throughout the winter, gradually becoming paler. Named after the Danish nurseryman.

Molinia caerulea **'Variegata'** (grass)
Height: Europe and USA 3ft (90cm).
Spread: 2ft (60cm).
Hardiness: Zone 5.
Deciduous.

Variegated leaves of yellow stripes that age white. A profusion of buff-coloured plumes in autumn that hold well into the winter.

Phalaris **'Arctic Sun'**
Height: Europe 2ft 6in (75cm); USA 2ft 6in (75cm).
Spread: will continue until contained.
Hardiness: Europe Zone 4; USA Zone 4.
Deciduous.

Relatively new introduction having golden variegated foliage. Not as vigorous as the species, and needs care in siting. Foliage can be cut back mid season to provide a fresh flush for later in the year. Dampish to average soil in sun or light shade.

Spodiopogon sibiricus Siberian Grey Beard (grass)
Height: Europe and USA 4ft (1.2m).
Spread: 3ft 3in (1m).
Hardiness: Europe Zone 3; USA Zone 4.
Deciduous.

Only one species of the family is cultivated for garden use. Produces a neat rounded form with almost horizontal leaves. Erect panicles of reddish brown flowers emerge in later summer, turning brown. Light shade with some moisture preferred but will tolerate deeper shade, although the form may be more lax. Leaves a deep red in the autumn.

Spodiopogon sibiricus **'West Lake'** This form has pinkish-red flower heads. Collected in China by Roy Lancaster and Hans Simon.

Medium Grasses for Damp Sites

When compiling a list of medium height grasses for damp conditions, it is always difficult to convey what exactly is damp. Obviously most average soils will have an element of moisture in them and where they are sheltered this will be greater through lack of evaporation, and they may be termed damp. The grasses I have listed here prefer the soil at least a little wetter than the above type; indeed, many will be quite happy in what may be termed a bog garden, with an element of water (as opposed to moisture) always

present. Other grasses, particularly the sedge family, may be happy with the amount of dampness available in a particular garden. It is really a matter of trial and, unfortunately, error to see what each individual site will sustain.

Acorus calamus Sweet Flag (Araceae)
Height: Europe and USA 4ft (1.2m).
Spread: Will continue until contained.
Hardiness: Zone 7.
Evergreen.

Although botanically not a grass, *Acorus* will fit into a green-orientated scheme. Upright iris-like leaves with a greenish yellow flower in sideways spikes. Sun or part shade. Bog or wet areas.

Carex elata **'Aurea'** Bowles Golden Sedge (sedge)
Height: Europe 2ft 6in (75cm); USA 2ft 6in (75cm).
Spread: 3ft (90cm).
Hardiness: Europe Zone 7; USA Zone 5.
Semi-evergreen.

One of the best sedges for part shade, its brilliant colour lifts shady spots. A graceful plant with golden deep yellow leaves. The colour is better when in sun, but still noteworthy if not a little greener in shade. Green stripe to edge of leaf. Growing from a tussock base, the leaves grow upright and then cascade down towards the ground. One of the older ornamental grasses being found as a sport on Wicken Fen, England by E. A. Bowles in 1885.

Carex Grayi Morning Star Sedge (sedge)
Height: Europe and USA 2ft 6in (75cm).
Spread: 18in (45cm).
Hardiness: Zone 5.
Deciduous.

Carex Grayi (Morning Star Sedge). The seed pods of this sedge are its main feature, star shaped green to begin with, turning brown as the season progresses.

Thin green leaves forming an upright shape, arching at the top. The seed heads are star-shaped pods that appear in late spring and are retained on the plant until autumn, when they turn brown. Named after Asa Gray, the American botanist.

Carex obnupta Slough Sedge (sedge)
Height: Europe 3–4ft (90cm–1.2m) USA 4ft (1.2m).
Spread: Will continue until contained.
Hardiness: Europe Zone 7; USA Zone 7.
Evergreen.

Large clumps of broadish green leaves with an attractive flower in mid summer, purplish black in colour. Will thrive in a moist to wet soil and can spread quickly in those conditions, being more restrained in a drier soil. A native of coastal California to British Columbia.

Carex pendula Pendulous Sedge (sedge)
Height: Europe 3ft (90cm); USA 3ft 3in (1m).
Spread: 3ft 3in (1m).
Hardiness: Europe Zone 8; USA Zone 8.
Evergreen.

A native to the UK and West and Central Europe and North Africa, pendula is often criticized for its ability to self-seed and survive, if not thrive, in most conditions, but placed in the right context, it can fill a number of requirements. Dense clumps of wide green foliage from a basal clump of about 60cm (2ft) from which a tall stem emerges with a dropping yellow catkin-type flower. Will grow successfully in sun or shade and both wet and dry soils, and often thrives quite happily in the cracks between paving and buildings in courtyards.

Carex pendula 'Moonraker'
With all the attributes of the above although not quite as vigorous. In spring, all the new foliage is a wonderful yellow colour that turns green as the season progresses.

Equisetum hyemale Horsetail (rush)
Height: Europe 5ft (1.5 m); USA 5ft (1.5m).
Spread: Will increase until confined.
Hardiness: Europe Zone 4; USA Zone 4.
Semi-evergreen.

This striking hollow-stemmed rush can provide a focal point in both natural plantings and modern garden design. Pencil-thick stems reach 1.5m in height, with vertical modal markings along their length, dark brown against the deep green of the stem. It should never be planted where it can spread unchecked as it is a vigorous colonizer, but quite happy in a large container or as a marginal planting. Will die back in harsh winters but quickly attain its full height the following season.

Juncus patens 'Carmen's Grey' (Californian grey rush). A typical sedge with upright cylindrical leaves, it performs well in the ground or containers.

Juncus patens 'Carmen's Grey' Californian Grey Rush (rush)
Height: Europe and USA 2ft (60cm).
Spread: 3ft 3in (1m).
Hardiness: Zone 7.
Evergreen.

Thin grey-leaved rush with very upright growth habit, forming dense clumps. Prefers a damp to wet soil, although once established it can cope with periods of drought. Flower heads typically rush-like, held near the top of the plant. Happy in containers. Selected by Ed Carmen in California.

Phalaris 'Arctic Sun'
Height: Europe 2ft 6in (75cm); USA 2ft 6in (75cm).
Spread: Will continue until contained.
Hardiness: Europe Zone 4; USA Zone 4.
Deciduous.

Relatively new introduction with golden variegated foliage. Not as vigorous as the species, and needs care in siting. Foliage can be cut back mid season to provide a fresh flush for later in the year. Dampish to average soil in sun or light shade.

Schoenoplectus lacustris subsp. Tabernaemontani 'Zebrinus' Common Clubrush (rush)
Height: 4ft (1.2m).
Spread: 5ft (1.5m).
Hardiness: Europe Zone 4; USA Zone 5. Deciduous.

The *Schoenoplectus* family are known as bulrushes, which causes confusion with the *Typha* species, which bears the same common name. The form 'Zebrinus' is also confused by some gardeners with *Miscanthus* 'Zebrinus', which of course prefers totally different growing conditions. Additionally, some of the *Scirpus* family have now been reclassified into this group.

Notwithstanding all this, *Schoenoplectus lacustris* makes a stunning addition to any wetland planting. Narrow round and upright stems are dark in colour with a very distinctive light yellow banding. Clump forming in habit and best grown in full sun either as a marginal or in a bog garden.

LOW-GROWING GRASSES

Low-growing grasses for sunny sites

Acorus gramineus 'Ogon' (Araceae)
Height: Europe 9in to 1ft (25 to 30cm); USA 1ft (30cm).
Spread: 1ft (30cm).
Hardiness: Europe Zone 5–7; USA Zone 5. Evergreen.

Slowly spreading mound of foliage curving outwards

Acorus gramineus 'Ogon'. Mound-forming with an open shape to the centre.

at its tips, often sparse in the middle of the plant. Colour can vary from gold-yellow to some cream leaves, perhaps due to cultural conditions or even due to the stock from which the plant originated. If in full sun, moist soil is required but will grow happily in containers.

Acorus gramineus 'Variegatus' A smaller version than 'Ogon' with creamy white and green striped foliage.

Carex buchananii Leather Leaf Sedge (sedge)
Height: Europe and USA 2ft (60cm).
Spread: 2ft (60cm).
Hardiness: Zone 7.
Evergreen.

Coppery bronze foliage forms erect mounds with very curled leaf tips. Originates in New Zealand. Makes an excellent container specimen. Good drainage is required for winter hardiness in cold areas.

Carex comans Hairy Sedge (sedge)
Height: Europe and USA 18in (45cm).
Spread: 4ft (1.2m).
Hardiness: Zone 7.
Evergreen.

An early bronze grass to be used in gardens. It has a very pendulous habit and becomes wider than it is tall. Dark bronze foliage in a mound. It can self-seed prolifically. Shows its form off well in tall containers, when the foliage can hang down instead of lying on the ground. Good drainage required. Hardy but short-lived, perhaps five years.

Acorus gramineus 'Variegatus' has creamy white-edged leaves, seen here with emerging seed heads.

Carex 'Frosted Curls' has arching foliage that is best shown off in a raised container.

Carex 'Frosted Curls' (sedge)
Height: Europe and USA 18in (45cm).
Spread: 3ft 3in (1m).
Hardiness: Zone 7.
Evergreen.

Of pendulous habit, the green foliage forms a wide mound that looks silver from a distance. As with *Carex comans*, it makes an excellent container specimen.

Some confusion has arisen as to its correct classification in the *Carex* family but it is still an attractive plant whatever its parentage.

Carex dipsacea (sedge)
Height: Europe 18in (45cm).
Spread: 18in (45cm).
Hardiness: Zone 7.
Evergreen.

Carex morrowii 'Ice Dance' is a value for money plant, evergreen, tough but elegant with a pretty seed head.

Dark bronze olive-green foliage which is best in full sun with the soil not too dry. Seed heads are almost black and carried within the foliage. Another of the New Zealand sedges.

Carex flagellifera 'Coca-cola' Mophead Sedge (sedge)
Height: Europe and USA 18in (45cm).
Spread: 3ft 3in (1m).
Hardiness: Zone 7.
Evergreen.

A habit not unlike *Carex comans*. Another brown sedge that has given rise to several selections such as 'Coca-cola', which has a soft brown colour. Sunny site with good drainage required.

Carex flava Yellow Sedge (sedge)
Height: Europe and USA
Spread: 2ft (60cm).
Hardiness: Zone 5.

Bright yellowish leaves. Flower heads orangey-brown in June and July, becoming globular and spiky.

Carex morrowii Kan Sage (sedge)
Height: Europe and USA 1ft (30cm).
Spread: 3ft 3in (1m).
Hardiness: Zone 5.
Evergreen.

Native to woodland of Japan, this sedge has a broadish leaf and forms mounds that slowly increase in spread. Several variegated forms have been developed for European gardens.

'Fisher's Form' Height: 1ft (30cm). A compact form with fresh yellow-white striped leaves, selected from Preedy Fisher's garden at Bromyard, England.

'Ice Dance' Height: 1ft (30cm). Slowly spreading habit, forming dense clumps. Dark green leaf with a pale creamy-white margin. Attractive spear-shaped seed head, dark brown with silver tip. Introduced into the USA from Japan by Barry Yinger.

'Silk Tassel' Height: 1ft (30cm). Wispy leaves striped white and green that may look silvery grey.

Carex oshimensis 'Evergold' has a mound-forming shape with bright foliage colour. An early introduction that has remained popular.

Carex oshimensis Oshima Kan Sage (sedge)
Height: Europe and USA 18in (45cm).
Spread: 2ft (60cm).
Hardiness: Zone 6.
Evergreen.

A native of Japan, it produces stiff leaves in a mound shape. It has given rise to variegated forms for garden cultivation.

'Evergold' Height: 18in (45cm). Green leaves have a central yellow stripe that ages cream. Forms a graceful cascading mound. Given to Blooms of Bressingham by the Royal Botanic Gardens at Kew.

Carex panacea Carnation Sedge (sedge)
Height: Europe and USA 10in (25cm).
Spread: Will continue until confined.
Hardiness: Zone 7.
Semi-evergreen.

Tussocks of gradually spreading glaucous blue foliage. Chocolate brown seed heads. Native of UK and Europe.

Carex pansa California Meadow Sedge (sedge)
Height: Europe 18in (45cm); USA 6in (15cm).
Spread: Will continue until confined.
Hardiness: Europe Zone 6; USA Zone 8.
Evergreen.

An alternative to lawn turf if the situation suits. Rich green foliage spreads by rhizomes to form a carpet but is not wildly invasive.

Carex praegracilis Western Meadow Sedge (sedge)
Height: Europe 18in (45cm); USA 2ft (60cm).

Spread: Will continue until confined.
Hardiness: Zone 5.
Evergreen.

Another alternative grass to traditional turf. Makes mats of dense evergreen foliage. Will tolerate a wide range of conditions from wet to dry and is a first class choice for green roofs. Will stand cutting to just a few inches.

Elymus magellanicus Blue Wheat Grass, Magellan Wheat Grass (grass)
Height: Europe 20in (50cm); USA 18in (45cm).
Spread: 18in (45cm).
Hardiness: Europe Zone 5; USA Zone 6.
Semi-evergreen.

Elymus magellanicus (Blue wheat grass) shows a brilliant silver colour and has a slightly untidy growth habit.

The bluest of all the blue grasses. Produces intense silvery blue foliage, upright growing but not tidily. Spreads by runners but very slowly, so does not cause a problem. A little choosy as to situation; it does not like humidity and high temperatures and is prone to develop rust in these conditions. Sunny site and good drainage for winter go a long way to solving the problems, plus a little light shade if in areas where humid conditions are possible. As with all the family, it does well in coastal areas.

Eragrostis spectabilis Purple Love Grass (grass)
Height: Europe and USA 2ft (60cm).
Spread: 3ft (90cm).
Hardiness: Zone 5.
Deciduous.

Well named as this grass produces a spectacular show of fine seed panicles, reddish purple in colour, so profuse that they appear like a cloud above the basal foliage. The foliage itself is not attractive, being a dull green and scruffy in its habit. Always prefers a sunny site on infertile, free-draining soil. Short-lived but can re-seed itself. A native of USA from Maine to Minnesota, south to Florida, Arizona and Mexico.

Festuca amethystina Tufted Fescue (grass)
Height: Europe and USA 2ft (60cm).
Spread: 1ft (30cm).
Hardiness: Zone 4.
Evergreen.

Typical fescue habit, with a basal clump of mid to dark greenish-blue leaves. Finely rolled leaves give a fine and delicate appearance. In June the flowers are held on gently pendulous stems, pinky-red in colour. The flowers themselves are purple tinted. Native of the Alps, Central Europe and Balkans. Prefers a free-draining soil.

Festuca glauca Blue Fescue (grass)
Height: Europe 1ft (30cm); USA 10in (25cm).
Spread: 2ft (60cm).
Hardiness: Europe Zone 5; USA Zone 4.
Evergreen.

A native of southern France, this is a widely-used garden plant, often seen as ground cover planting. Neat, clump forming foliage, very tufty in appearance and blue in colour. Seed heads are held above the plant on stems that are blue grey but fade to a straw colour. If the foliage shape and colour are the main attractions, the seed heads could be cut off. Can be short-lived, four years or so, and deteriorates in the centre of the clump if not maintained. Prefers a free-draining soil and sunny position. Produces viable but variable seed so care should be taken if the original strain is desired.

'Elijah Blue' A reliable form, perhaps still the bluest and best growing.

'Siskiyou Blue' Height: 20in (50cm). A more drooping form and slightly taller than the other varieties.

Festuca idahoensis Idaho Fescue, Blue Bunchgrass (grass)
Height: Europe 2ft (60cm); USA 14in (35cm).
Spread: 2ft (60cm).
Hardiness: Europe Zone 4; USA Zone 5.
Evergreen.

Tight clumps of silvery blue-grey leaves, the colour extending into the flower stems. Thought to be longer lived and not as prone to central dieback as *Festuca glauca*. Prefers a sunny, open site with good drainage. Despite its name, the actual home range of the plant is from British Columbia to Alberta, south to central California and Colorado.

'Tomales Bay' Height: 15in (40cm). A selection with good steely-blue foliage and a drought resistant capacity.

Festuca glauca 'Elijah Blue'. A neat mound-forming grass, perhaps still the bluest of the Festucas.

Hakonechloa macra (Hakone grass). A very graceful form of grass seen here as a mass planting alongside a path at RHS Garden Wisley.

Hakonechloa macra Hakone Grass (grass)
Height: Europe 18in (45cm); USA 1ft to 3ft (30cm to 90cm).
Spread: 3ft 3in (1m).
Hardiness: Europe Zone 5; USA Zone 4. Deciduous.

A very graceful grass producing arching stems of a rich green colour. Flowers are dainty but not a main feature of the plant. If grown in hot climates it is best given a little shade, where it will grow well. A favourite for under the edge of tree canopies. In cooler climates, it is happy in full sun. Spreads by rhizomes but is not rampant. Prefers a little moisture in the soil but not heavy soils. A native of Japan, including the area around Mount Hakone, hence its common name.

Hakonechloa macra 'Aureola'. A beautiful arching habit and good colour makes a fantastic shape in a pot if kept out of full sun.

'Aureola' (Albo-aurea) Probably the most seen of all the cultivars. Elegant gold and green striped foliage that grows in a mound form. If in sun, some moisture is essential in the soil and the colour may not be as rich as when grown in its preferred conditions of part shade. Excellent in a pot where the foliage cascades down.

***Imperata cylindrica* 'Konigensis'** (grass)
Height: Europe 2ft (60cm); USA 2ft 3in (70cm).
Spread: Will continue until contained.
Hardiness: Zone 6.
Deciduous.

The parent plant of the much admired 'Red Baron' (see below). In tropical climates, its vigorous growth has caused problems. This, however, is the variety 'Konengis.'

***Imperata cylindrica rubra* 'Red Baron'** (Japanese Blood Grass)With stunning red variegation spreading from the leaf tips down the pale green stem, this is an attractive garden plant. In temperate climates, it is very slow spreading but in warmer zones can show an aggressive spreading tendency. Best grown in a sunny site with underlying moisture but not too wet for the winter in colder areas. Often grown in a container in the colder parts of the UK to help establishment and control conditions, and it makes an ideal subject.

Luzula sylvatica Greater Woodrush (rush)
Height: Europe 18in (45cm); USA 2ft (60cm).
Spread: 3ft 3in (1m).
Hardiness: Europe Zone 6; USA Zone 4.
Evergreen.

Imperata cylindrical rubra 'Red Baron'. A stunning red colour developing over the season. It likes a sunny site with a moist soil.

Although the largest of the woodrush family, it is happiest in shade or part shade. It will cope with a sunny position providing there is sufficient moisture in the soil. Makes an excellent ground cover plant with wide, dark green leaves forming rosettes of clumpy growth. Native of UK, South, West and Central Europe.

Nassella trichotoma Serrated Tussock Grass (grass)
Height: Europe and USA 18in (45cm).
Spread: 3ft 3in (1m).
Hardiness: Zone 7.
Evergreen.

Neat mounds of hair-like bright green foliage. Airy structured flower heads with tiny purplish brown spikelets. Sunny, well drained site. In warmer climates of the USA and Australia, it has become a noxious weed but in cooler climates such as the UK this is not the case. Native of Argentina and Uruguay.

Ophiopogon japonicus minor Mondo Grass (Liliacaea)
Height: Europe 4in (10cm); USA 4in (10cm).
Spread: 1ft (30cm).
Hardiness: Europe Zone 6; USA Zone 6.
Evergreen.

Although botanically not a grass, the tough strap-like leaves of this plant make it useful in a grass scheme.

Slow-growing, miniature evergreen leaves form a small, tight clump. Useful as ground cover but not for large areas because of its slow growth habit. Occasionally produces a pink flower.

Ophiopogon planiscapus 'Nigrescens' Height: 8in (20cm). Mound-forming with strappy black leaves and whitish flowers followed by a black berry. In view of its unique black colour it is widely used in modern landscape and urban garden schemes. Sun or part shade.

Pennisetum alopecuroides 'Little Bunny' (grass)
Height: Europe and USA 18in (45cm).
Spread: 18in (45cm).
Hardiness: Zone 6.
Deciduous.

A truly miniature version of the fountain grass. This selection from Hameln has all the characteristics of a mound-forming variety with green foliage turning to golden yellow in autumn, The flowers are foxtail in shape and fluffy, held above the plant's foliage. Flowers pinkish on opening then fading to beige by late summer, and retained into winter. Sunny site with a free-draining soil. Flowers not produced as freely in wet, colder climates.

'Little Honey' A sport from 'Little Bunny'. All the same characteristics are retained but with the added attraction of finely variegated leaves of white and green. Introduced by Cliff Russell's son Alan at Richboro, USA.

Ophiopogon planiscapus 'Nigrescens' is not a true grass as it produces a small flower and berry. It is very useful in garden design because of its unique colour.

Pennisetum orientale

Oriental Fountain Grass
(grass)
Height: Europe 2ft (60cm);
USA 2ft (60cm).
Spread: 2ft (60cm).
Hardiness: Europe Zone 6;
USA Zone 6.
Deciduous.

Not as vigorous in growth as *Pennisetum alopecuroides* when grown in cooler climates but still worth space in the garden. Mounds of grey green foliage with the characteristic foxtail shaped flowers, pinkish on opening and fading to white through the season. Sunny site with free draining soil. Can be grown in part shade in warmer climates than the UK. Originated from North Africa to Iran, Caucasus and Central Asia.

Poa colensoi New Zealand Blue Grass (grass)
Height: Europe and USA 1ft (30cm).
Spread: 2ft (60cm).
Hardiness: Zone 7.
Evergreen.

Erect, slightly arching, pale to intense blue leaves. Flowers sparse and vary in colour from greenish to bluish, fading to a pale brown. Foliage very fine in texture, similar to a Fescue. Native of New Zealand.

Sesleria caerulea (Blue moor grass). Has a neat mound forming shape and blue foliage.

Sesleria caerulea Blue Moor Grass (grass)
Height: Europe 6in (15cm); USA 8in (20cm).
Spread: 1ft (30cm).
Hardiness: Europe Zone 7; USA Zone 4.
Evergreen.

Native to the UK and Europe, a much underrated grass. A basal mound of foliage is glaucous blue on the upper side and dark green on the underside, and as both sides can be seen at the same time, the overall impression is of a blue hue. Small spikes of flowers are produced on short stems. Dark at the beginning with golden pollen sacs, they become green with age and loss of pollen and then fade to a straw colour. A useful grass for green roofs due to its drought tolerance.

Sporobolus heterolepis Prairie Dropseed (grass)
Height: Europe and USA 2ft 6in (75cm).
Spread: 1m (3ft 3in).
Hardiness: Zone 4.
Deciduous.

Fine-textured mounds of free-flowing foliage, not stiff in appearance. Medium green foliage in summer turns to a deep orange and then fades to a light copper colour throughout the autumn months. The flower panicles are dark green with papery blackish to purple larger parts. Unusually the plant is faintly scented. Although slow to mature, it is long-lived and happy on a wide range of soils including clay. Prefers full sun. A native of the North American prairies.

'Tara' Height: 2ft (60cm). Slightly stiffer foliage with good orange-red colour in autumn and a compact habit.

'Wisconsin' A selection chosen for reliable bloom in Europe. Selected by Hans Simon from plant material of Wisconsin provenance.

Uncinia rubra Red Hook Sedge (sedge)
Height: Europe 2ft (60cm); USA 1ft 2in (35cm).
Spread: 2ft (60cm).
Hardiness: Zone 8.
Evergreen.

Narrow dark red to bronze-green leaves form a neat tussock. Insignificant flowers turn into hooks, hence the name. Sunny site for best colour and not too dry in the summer months. In colder areas, it is not the hardiest of plants in a severe winter.

Low-growing grasses for part shade

Acorus gramineus 'Ogon' (Araceae)
Height: Europe 10in–1ft (25–30cm); USA 1ft (30cm).
Spread: 1ft (30cm).
Hardiness: Europe Zone 5–7; USA Zone 5.
Evergreen.

Slowly spreading mound of foliage curving outwards at its tips, often sparse in the middle of the plant. Colour can vary from gold yellow to some cream leaves, perhaps due to cultural conditions or even due to the stock from which the plant originated. If in full sun, moist soil is required but will grow happily in containers.

Acorus gramineus 'Variegatus' A smaller version than 'Ogon' with creamy white and green striped foliage.

Briza media Quaking Grass, Tottergrass, Jiggle-joggles, Rattle Grass (grass)
Height: Europe 2ft (60cm); USA 2ft 6in (75cm).
Spread: 2ft (60cm).
Hardiness: Europe Zone 5; USA Zone 4.
Semi-evergreen.

The wide range of common names indicates the familiarity with this native grass for many years. From a tight mound of green foliage, many delicate heads are sent up to about 2ft (60cm). As they dry, they become golden in colour and dance in the slightest breeze. From their emergence in May, they will be retained throughout the summer. Prefers a free draining soil and sunny site but will tolerate some shade and a clayish soil.

Briza media 'Golden Bee' A selected form of the above, perhaps with a larger seed head and more golden colour.

Carex dipsacea (sedge)
Height: Europe and USA 18in (45cm).
Spread: 18in (45cm).
Hardiness: Zone 7.
Evergreen.

Dark bronze olive-green foliage, which is best in full sun with the soil not too dry. Seed heads are almost black and carried within the foliage. Another of the New Zealand sedges.

Carex elata 'Aurea' Bowles Golden Sedge (sedge)
Height: Europe 2ft 6in (75cm); USA 2ft 8in (80cm).
Spread: 3ft (90cm).
Hardiness: Europe Zone 7; USA Zone 5.
Semi-evergreen.

One of the best sedges for part shade, its brilliant colour lifting a shady spot. A graceful plant with golden deep yellow leaves. The colour is better when in sun but still noteworthy if not a little greener in shade. Green stripe to edge of leaf. Growing from a tussock base, the leaves grow upright and then cascade down towards the ground. One of the older ornamental grasses being found as a sport on Wicken Fen, England by E. A. Bowles in 1885.

Carex elata 'Knightshayes' (sedge)
Height: Europe and USA 2ft (60cm).
Spread: 3ft (90cm).
Hardiness: Europe Zone 7; USA Zone 5.
Deciduous.

A sport of 'Aurea', this variety has completely golden leaves as opposed to the green stripe on the edge carried by 'Aurea'. Forming a graceful arching clump, the flower heads are dark brown to blackish, fading to buff. Performs best in part shade with a moisture retentive soil. Named after the nursery that introduced it, Knightshayes Court, Devon.

Carex oshimensis 'Evergold'
Height: 1ft 4in (40cm).
Spread: 2ft (60cm).
Hardiness: Europe Zone 5; USA Zone 5.
Evergreen.

Green leaves have a central yellow stripe that ages to cream. Forms a graceful cascading mound. Given to Blooms of Bressingham by the Royal Botanic Gardens at Kew.

Carex flava Yellow Sedge (sedge)
Height: Europe 2ft (60cm); USA 2ft (60cm).
Spread: 2ft (60cm).
Hardiness: Europe Zone 5; USA Zone 5.
Semi-evergreen.

Bright yellowish leaves. Flowerheads orangey-brown in June and July, becoming globular and spiky.

Carex morrowii 'Fisher's Form'
Height: 1ft (30cm).
Spread: 2ft (60cm).
Hardiness:
Evergreen.

A compact form with fresh yellow-white striped leaves from Preedy Fisher's garden at Bromyard, England.

Carex morrowii 'Ice Dance' Height: 30cm (1ft) Slowly spreading habit forming dense clumps. Dark green leaf with a pale creamy white margin. Attractive seed head, spear shaped, dark brown with silver tip. Introduced by Barry Yinger into the USA from Japan.

Carex morrowii 'Ice Dance' has strappy leaves with cream edges, and is mound-forming in shape.

Carex oshimensis 'Evergold' is a neat mound-forming sedge.

Carex muskingumensis Palm Sedge (sedge)
Height: Europe and USA 2ft (60cm).
Spread: 3ft 3in (1m).
Hardiness: Europe Zone 7; USA Zone 4.
Semi-evergreen.

Narrow green leaves tapering to a point radiate from a lax stem. Very architectural shape with a clump-forming habit. Flower heads are light brown in colour, interesting when viewed closely but not standing out in the overall view of the plant. Native of woodlands in North and Central America. Prefers a moist site and does best in light shade, although it will grow in sun.

'Little Midge' Height: 6in (15cm). A dwarf form of the above and an exact replica in miniature.

'Oehme' Leaves have thin yellow margins in the spring turning green as the season progresses. Same size as muskingumensis but best grown in light shade.

Carex Muskingumensis 'Oehme'. Leaves edged yellow are on this form of Palm sedge.

'Silberstreif' A slightly more compact form than muskingumensis, height 50cm. Foliage variegated with a yellow and green stripe. Best grown in part shade.

Carex panacea Carnation Sedge (sedge)
Height: Europe 10in (25cm); USA 10in (25cm).
Spread: Will continue until confined.
Hardiness: Europe Zone 7; USA Zone 7.
Semi evergreen.

Tussocks of gradually-spreading glaucous blue foliage. Chocolate brown seed heads. Native of UK and Europe.

Carex praegracilis Western Meadow Sedge (sedge)
Height: Europe 18in (45cm); USA 1ft (30cm).
Spread: Will continue until confined.
Hardiness: Europe Zone 5; USA Zone 5.
Evergreen.

Another alternative grass to traditional turf. Makes mats of dense evergreen foliage. Will tolerate a wide range of conditions from wet to dry and is a first class choice for green roofs. Will stand cutting to just a few inches.

Carex testacea Orange Sedge (sedge)
Height: Europe 18in (45cm); USA 18in (45cm).
Spread: 18in (45cm).
Hardiness: Europe Zone 7; USA Zone 6.
Evergreen.

A very attractive and neat plant arching gracefully towards its top. The foliage is green at the base, changing to a pleasant strong orange colour at the top of the plant. This orange colour intensifies throughout the season, especially when it is planted in a sunny position. A very good plant for containers as it is not too large and its arching habit is more pronounced when it is clear of the ground. Round seed heads borne on dropping stems that touch the ground. Another native sedge of New Zealand.

Carex tenuiculmis Brown Sedge (sedge)
Height: Europe 2ft (60cm); USA 2ft (60cm).
Spread: 3ft 3in (1m).
Hardiness: Europe Zone 6; USA Zone 6.
Evergreen.

Attractive habit, arching gently at the top and so not laying on the ground. Chocolate coloured foliage containing a range of reds and browns. Happy in sun or part shade. Originated in New Zealand.

Hakonechloa macra, seen here turning into its autumn foliage with its delicate seed heads still visible.

Hakonechloa macra Hakone Grass (grass)
Height: Europe 18in (45cm); USA 1–3ft (30–90cm).
Spread: 3ft 3in (1m).
Hardiness: Europe Zone 5; USA Zone 4.
Deciduous.

A very graceful grass producing arching stems of a rich green colour. Flowers are dainty but not a main feature of the plant. If grown in hot climates, it is best given a little shade where it will grow well. A favourite for under the edge of tree canopies. In cooler climates, it is happy in full sun. Spreads by rhizomes but not rampant. Prefers a little moisture in the soil but not heavy soils. A native of Japan including the area around Mount Hakone, hence its common name.

***Hakonechloa macra* 'Aureola'** (albo-aurea)
Probably the most common of all the cultivars. Elegant
gold and green striped foliage that grows in a mound
form. If grown in the sun, some moisture is essential
in the soil and the colour may not be as rich as when
grown in its preferred conditions of part shade.
Excellent in a pot where the foliage cascades down.

***Juncus effusus* 'Spiralis'** Corkscrew Rush (rush)
Height: Europe 18in (45cm); USA 14in (35cm).
Spread: 2ft (60cm).
Hardiness: Europe Zone 4; USA Zone 5.
Evergreen.

A natural sport of the soft rush. Stems spiral upwards
and outwards, often being quite tight in their form like
a corkscrew. Dark green in colour and glossy, like most
rushes it grows rapidly. Prefers some moisture and
can be grown as a marginal. The plant does well as an
unusual container plant as long as it is kept moist. Sun
or part shade. Found in Connemara, Ireland, by David
Bishop of Belfast.

***Juncus inflexus* 'Afro'** Blue Madonna (rush)
Height: Europe 1ft (30cm); USA 14in (35cm).
Spread: 2ft (60cm).
Hardiness: Europe Zone 4; USA Zone 6.
Evergreen.

A form of the hard rush not dissimilar in habit to
'Spiralis' but perhaps not as twisted. Bluish green in
colour. Prefers moisture in some form, either damp
soil or as a marginal aquatic, but if used as the latter it
would be better removed from the water during the
winter months. Will grow happily in a container in sun
or part shade.

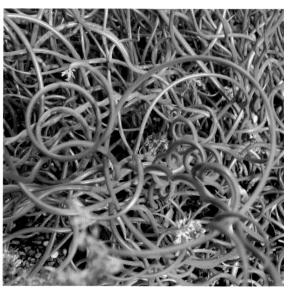

Juncus inflexus 'Afro' (Blue Madonna) has a bluish green
foliage, and is less tight in its curls than spiralis.

***Juncus patens* 'Carmen's Grey'** Californian Grey
Rush (rush)
Height: Europe 2ft (60cm); USA 2ft (60cm).
Spread: 3ft 3in (1m).
Hardiness: Europe Zone 7; USA Zone 7.
Evergreen.

Juncus effusus 'Spiralis' (Corkscrew rush). An unusual form of
rush that does well in containers or the ground as long as it
has moisture.

Thin grey-leaved rush with very upright growth habit forming dense clumps. Prefers damp to wet soil, although once established, it can cope with periods of drought. Flowerheads typical rush-like held near the top of the plant. Happy in containers. Selected by Ed Carmen at California.

Luzula nivea (Snowy woodrush). Showing its white flowers, this is perhaps the closest an ornamental grass gets to a flowerhead. It brightens a shady spot.

Juncus patens 'Carmen's Grey' (Californian grey rush) has an upright habit and the typical small flowers of a rush.

Luzula nivea Snowy Woodrush (rush)
Height: Europe and USA 2ft (60cm).
Spread: 1ft (30cm).
Hardiness: Europe Zone 5; USA Zone 6.
Evergreen.

Basal clump of dark green leaves covered in silvery hairs. Flowers borne on initially upright stems which become pendulous with age. Flower inflorescences bright white fading with age. Native of Central and Southern Europe. Prefers shade.

Luzula sylvatica Greater Woodrush (rush)
Height: Europe 18in (45cm); USA 2ft (60cm).
Spread: 3ft 3in (1m).
Hardiness: Europe Zone 6; USA Zone 4.
Evergreen.

Although the largest of the woodrush family, it is happiest in shade or part shade. It will cope with a sunny position providing there is sufficient moisture in the soil. Makes an excellent ground cover plant with wide, dark green leaves forming rosettes of clumpy growth. Native of UK, South, West and Central Europe.

Luzula sylvatica 'Aurea' (rush)
Height: Europe and USA 18in (45cm).
Spread: 3ft 3in (1m).
Hardiness: Zone 6.
Evergreen.

A golden-leaved version of the Great Woodrush. Gold foliage in rosettes that form neat mounds. In winter the colour changes to a bright yellow. Red seed heads are held just clear of the plant in the spring. Any soil suitable, but prefers some moisture to be present. The plant does better in shade than full sun, where the leaves can get scorched in the summer.

Luzula sylvatica 'Hohe Tatra' showing its profusion of seed heads, which are held just above the foliage.

Luzula sylvatica 'Hohe tatra' Very similar in habit and colour to 'Aurea' and is sometimes confused, but 'Hohe tatra' has broader leaves and is more pendulous in habit than *sylvatica* 'Aurea', which look slightly more spiky in appearance. Prefers shade. The plant hails from the Tatra Mountains between Poland and Slovakia.

Melica uniflora 'Variegata'. A beautifully delicately marked plant with attractive small seed heads.

Melica uniflora Wood Melick (grass)
Height: Europe and USA 1ft (30cm).
Spread: 1ft (30cm).
Hardiness: Zone 7.
Deciduous.

Native of the UK, Europe, Turkey, Northern Iran and Caucasus. Its delicate leaf forms an open clump by creeping roots, although it is not vigorous enough to be invasive. Delicate-looking seed heads, purple brown on a purplish stem. Shady woodland type of site preferred.

Melica uniflora 'Variegata' A little more compact than the species. Green and white striped leaves provide a focal point in shady woodland settings. Foliage attains a pinkish hue during the season, adding to the delicate attractiveness of the plant. Shady site preferred.

Melica nutans Nodding Melick (grass)
Height: Europe and USA 2ft (60cm).
Spread: 2ft (60cm).
Hardiness: Zone 7.
Deciduous.

Delicate-looking bright green leaves, slender in appearance, turning yellow in the autumn. Flowers are held on slightly drooping stems above the plant and are pinkish violet in colour with pale yellow stamens when mature. Native to Europe through to Russia, China and Japan. Shady site required.

Milium effusum 'Aureum' Bowles Golden Grass (grass)
Height: Europe 1ft (30cm); USA 18in (45cm).
Spread: 1ft (30cm).
Hardiness: Zone 6.
Deciduous.

Known as Bowles Golden Grass (not to be confused with *Carex elata* 'Aurea', which is Bowles Golden Sedge). New spring foliage is very bright, clear golden yellow and this extends to all parts of the plant. Open flower panicles borne within and just above the plant add interest but are not a major feature. Fades to pale as the season progresses. Best in light shade in cooler climates to retain its bright yellow colour. Has a mild tendency to self-seed around the garden. It can be cut back mid-season to prevent this and encourage new growth. Introduced by E. A. Bowles from the Birmingham Botanic Garden, England.

Milium effusum 'Aureum' (Bowles golden grass) has a lovely deep yellow colour early in the season, fading with time, and nice golden seed heads of same colour stems.

Milium effusum aureum 'Yaffle' A selection with bright green leaves striped down the centre by a number of yellow lines. Has retained the bright golden flowers of 'Aureum' that are held above the plant. Same habit and conditions as its parent.

Ophiopogon japonicus minor Mondo Grass (Liliacaea)
Height: Europe 4in (10cm); USA 4in (10cm).
Spread: 1ft (30cm).
Hardiness: Europe Zone 6, USA Zone 6.
Evergreen.

Although botanically not a grass, the tough strap-like leaves of this plant make it useful in a grass scheme. Slow growing miniature form of evergreen leaves

forming a small tight clump. Useful as ground cover but because of its slow growth habit, not for large areas. Occasionally produces a pink flower.

Ophiopogon planiscapus 'Nigrescens' Height: 8in (20cm). Mound-forming with strappy black leaves and whitish flowers followed by a black berry. In view of its unique black colour it is widely used in modern landscape and urban garden schemes. Sun or part shade.

Sesleria caerulea (Blue moor grass) has a neat leaf that never becomes straggly. It keeps its blue colour throughout the season.

Sesleria caerulea Blue Moor Grass (grass)
Height: Europe 6in (15cm); USA 8in (20cm).
Spread: 1ft (30cm).
Hardiness: Europe Zone 7; USA Zone 4.
Evergreen.

Native to the UK and Europe, a much underrated grass. A basal mound of foliage, which is glaucous blue on the upper side and dark green on the underside. As both sides can be seen at the same time, the overall impression is of a blue hue. Small spikes of flowers are produced on short stems. Dark at the beginning with golden pollen sacs, they become green with age and loss of pollen and then fade to a straw colour. A useful grass to use on green roofs due to its drought tolerance.

Uncinia rubra Red Hook Sedge (sedge)
Height: Europe 2ft (60cm); USA 14in (35cm).
Spread: 2ft (60cm).
Hardiness: Europe Zone 8; USA Zone 8.
Evergreen.

Narrow dark red to bronze green leaves form a neat tussock. Insignificant flowers that turn into hooks, hence the name. Provide a sunny site for best colour, but not too dry in the summer months. In colder areas, it is not the hardiest of plants in a severe winter.

Low-growing grasses for damp sites

Acorus gramineus 'Ogon' (Araceae)
Height: Europe 10in–1ft (25–30cm); USA 1ft (30cm).
Spread: 1ft (30cm).
Hardiness: Europe Zone 5–7; USA Zone 5.
Evergreen.

Slowly spreading mound of foliage curving outwards at its tips, often sparse in the middle of the plant. Colour can vary from gold yellow to some cream leaves, perhaps due to cultural conditions or even due to the stock from which the plant originated. If in full sun, moist soil is required but will grow happily in containers.

Acorus gramineus 'Variegatus' A smaller version than 'Ogon' with creamy white and green striped foliage.

Carex muskingumensis Palm Sedge (sedge)
Height: Europe and USA 2ft (60cm).
Spread: 3ft 3in (1m).
Hardiness: Europe Zone 7; USA Zone 4.
Semi-evergreen.

Narrow green leaves tapering to a point radiate from a lax stem. Very architectural shape with a clump forming habit. Flowerheads are light brown in colour, interesting when viewed closely but not standing out in the overall view of the plant. Native of woodlands in North and Central America. Prefers a moist site and does best in light shade, although it will grow in sun.

Carex muskingumensis 'Little Midge' Height: 15cm (6in). A dwarf form of the above and an exact replica in miniature.

Carex muskingumensis 'Oehme' Leaves have thin yellow margins in the spring turning green as the season progresses. Same size as muskingumensis but best grown in light shade.

Isolepis cernua Mop Sedge, Fibre Optic Plant (sedge)
Height: Europe and USA 6in (15cm).
Spread: 1ft (30cm).
Hardiness: Zone 8.
Semi-evergreen.

The common name derives from the fibre optic lamps that were popular in the 1970s. It has hair-like green stems that form a mop-like clump terminating in a small spike, whitish in colour. Best grown in a pot or an elevated planting so that the foliage habit can be shown off to its best advantage. Prefers some moisture at all times. Part shade suits but will cope with sun if the moisture is present.

Isolepis cernua (Mop sedge) has a lovely green colour with little pale seed heads on the tips of its leaves.

Juncus effusus 'Spiralis' Corkscrew Rush (rush)
Height: Europe 18in (45cm); USA 14in (35cm).
Spread: 2ft (60cm).
Hardiness: Europe Zone 4; USA Zone 5.
Evergreen.

A natural sport of the soft rush. Stems spiral upwards
and outwards often being quite tight in their form like
a corkscrew. Dark green in colour and glossy, it grows
rapidly like most rushes. Prefers some moisture and
can be grown as a marginal. The plant does well as
an unusual container plant as long as it is kept moist.
Sun or part shade. Found by David Bishop of Belfast in
Connemara, Ireland.

Juncus inflexus 'Afro' Blue Madonna (rush)
Height: Europe 1ft (30cm); USA 14in (35cm).
Spread: 2ft (60cm).
Hardiness: Europe Zone 4; USA Zone 6.
Evergreen.

A form of the hard rush not dissimilar to the habit of
'Spiralis', but perhaps not as twisted. Bluish green in
colour. Prefers moisture in some form, either damp
soil or as a marginal aquatic but if used as the latter, it
would be better removed from the water during the
winter months. Will grow happily in a container in sun
or part shade.

Juncus patens 'Carmen's Grey' Californian Grey
Rush (rush)
Height: Europe 2ft (60cm); USA 2ft (60cm).
Spread: 3ft 3in (1m).
Hardiness: Europe Zone 7; USA Zone 7.
Evergreen.

Thin grey leaved rush with very upright growth habit
forming dense clumps. Prefers a damp to wet soil,
although once established, it can cope with periods of
drought. Flowerheads typical rush-like held near the
top of the plant. Happy in containers. Selected by Ed
Carmen at California.

Rhynonchaspora latifolia White Top Star Sedge
(sedge)
Height: Europe 18in (45cm); USA 2ft 8in (80cm).
Spread: 1ft (30cm).
Hardiness: Zone 8.
Deciduous.

Juncus effusus 'Spiralis' (Corkscrew rush) is mound-forming
and will grow happily as a marginal planting in water.

Aptly named Star Sedge. Sometimes mistaken for
a flower head, the star is in fact the bracts of the
plant. Six to ten are produced in a star shape, white
at the base running to green at the tips, held on
thin green stems with thin green leaves. Best grown
as a pond marginal or in a bog garden, but can also
be grown in a container providing enough moisture
is available. Not particularly hardy in the northern
regions of the UK.

Typha minima Miniature Cat-tail (cat-tail)
Height: Europe 2ft 2in (65cm); USA 2ft 8in (80cm).
Spread: 2ft 6in (75cm).
Hardiness: Europe Zone 6; USA Zone 5.
Deciduous.

A miniature cat-tail ideal for small ponds or water
features. Bright green leaves and male and female
flowers held on 60cm stems with a slight gap
between the two. Both are dark brown and the
female part is oval and nearly round in shape. Must
have moisture but will take sun or light shade.

Glossary

Annual: a plant that completes its entire life cycle in one year.

Anther: the pollen-producing part of the male flower organ, located at the top of the slender stalk.

Awl: a slender bristle-like or needle-like appendage extending from a bract. Awls may be short or many inches long, contributing to the beauty of grass flowers.

Blade: the flat part of a leaf as opposed to the petiole.

Bract: modified leafy structure accompanying an inflorescence and often occurring on the flowering stem.

Caespitose: tufted, clump-forming.

Capsule: dry fruit containing seed.

Culm: the above-ground stem of grasses, including bamboos.

Deciduous: a plant that sheds all its leaves annually.

Evergreen: a plant retaining all its foliage throughout the year.

Floret: in grasses, the collective term for an individual flower plus the inner and outer bract.

Glaucous: bluish green.

Herbaceous: any plant whose above-ground parts are soft, not woody.

Hispid: bristly, covered with short hairs.

Inflorescence: the flowering portion of a plant.

Internode: the section of a culm between two nodes.

Keel: narrow ridge occurring along the midrib of a leaf.

Lanceolate: three to four times as long as wide and tapering gradually towards the tip.

Ligule: a thin flap of tissue at the top of the leaf sheath.

Monoculture: a planting of one type of plant.

Monoecious: having separate male and female flowers on the same plant.

Node: the point on a stem from which a leaf grows, the joint on the stems of grasses and bamboos.

Panicle: term used for the flower head of a grass.

Perennial: a plant that grows and reproduces for many years.

Petiole: a leaf stalk.

Raceme: a kind of inflorescence with many stalked flowers on a single axis.

Rhizome: a stem that grows along under the ground bearing buds that produce shoots.

Runner: a stem that grows along the ground and produces new plants at its nodes.

Sheath: the lower part of the leaf, originating at a node, that clasps and encircles the stem.

Spike: an inflorescence composed of numerous stalkless flowers arranged on a single axis.

Sport: an individual plant showing marked variation from the normal type.

Stolon: a stem that grows along the ground.

Terminal: located at the top or end.

Tussock: a thick tuft.

Umbel: an inflorescence in which all the flower stalks arise together from a central plant.

Viriparus: of plants, bearing young plants that can take root and when detached, assume an independent existence.

Woody: having well-developed secondary tissue as is present in trees and shrubs.

Appendix I
Grasses for specific sites and uses

Although the book is set out with a view to guiding the reader quickly to the relevant section, the following lists contain grasses for specific uses and sites that do not fall into the categories used in the main text.

Annual grasses

Agrostis nebulosa
Aira elegantissima
Apera spica-venti
Avena sterilis
Briza maxima
Bromus macrostachys
Bromus madritensis
Catapodium rigidum
Cynosurus echinatus
Echinochloa crus-galli
Lagurus ovatus
Lagurus ovatus nana
Lamarckia aurea
Lolium temulentum
Lophochloa cristata
Panicum capillare
Panicum miliaceum
Pennisetum sectaceum
Phalaris canariensis
Phalaris minor
Phleum paniculatum
Setaria glauca
Setaria macrostachys
Setaria pumila
Sorghum bicolour
Sorghum nigrum
Zea mays

Ornamental British natives (including varieties found as sports and introduced to the market)

Agostia canina
Agostia gigantea
Ammophila arenaria
Anthroxanthum odoratum
Apera spica-venti
Briza media
Bromus (several of the species)
Calamagrostis epigejos
Carex elata 'Aurea'
Carex elata aurea 'Knightshayes'
Carex flacca
Carex panacea
Carex pendula
Carex pendula 'Moonraker'
Carex riparia
Cyperus longas
Deschampsia flexuosa
Eriophorum
Festuca arundinacea
Glyceria maxima
Hordeum jubatum (naturalized)
Isolepis cernua
Juncus (all the species)
Koeleria cistata
Lagurus ovatus
Leymus arenarius
Luzula sylvatica
Luzula pilosa
Milium effusum
Molinia caerulea ssp. caerulea
Molinia caerulea ssp. arundinacea
Phleum pratense
Schoenoplectus
Stipa pennata
Typha angustifolia

Grasses suitable for seaside gardens

Ammophila arenaria
Ampelodesmos mauritanicus
Bromus intermis
Calamagrostis nutkaensis
Carex testacea
Chasmanthium latifolium
Cortaderia fulvida
Cortaderia Richardii
Cortaderia selloana
Helictotrichon sempervirens
Hordeum jubatum
Leymus arenarius
Lygeum spartum
Oryza sativa
Panicum virgatum
Phalaris arundinacea and cultivars
Phragmites australis and cultivars
Spartina pectinata
Sporobolus virginicus
Triticum aestivum
Uniola latifolia

In addition, it may be possible to grow some of the deciduous grasses as they will die back in the winter and therefore miss most of the salt-laden winds that may be a problem in winter. Species with thin leaves would be best suited; however, tall grasses that die back but retain all their foliage in a dead state may well be worth considering. This could include any of the Miscanthus or Panicum species.

Appendix 2
Common names of grasses

African love grass – *Eragrostis curvula*

Albardine – *Lygeum spartum*

Autumn moor grass – *Sesleria autumnalis*

Big blue stem – *Andropogon gerardii*

Blood grass – *Imperata cylindrica* 'Rubra'

Blue hair grass – *Koeleria glauca*

Blue lyme grass – *Leymus arenarius*

Blue moor grass – *Sesleria caerulea*

Blue oat grass – *Helictotrichon sempervirens*

Blue wheat grass – *Elymus hispidus*

Bottle-brush grass – *Hystrix patula*

Bowles golden sedge – *Carex elata* 'Aurea'

Bowles golden grass – *Milium effusum aureum*

Brome grass – *Bromus* ssp.

Buchanan's brown sedge – *Carex Buchananii*

Bulbous oat grass – *Arrhenatherum elatus bulbosum variegatum*

Bulrush – *Schoenoplectus lacustris*

Bunny tails – *Lagurus ovatus nanus*

Cat-tails – *Typha* ssp.

Cloud grass – *Agrostis nebulosa*

Common quaking grass – *Briza media*

Common reed – *Phragmites australis*

Corkscrew rush – *Juncus effusus* 'Spiralis'

Corn – *Zea mays*

Cotton grass – *Eriophorum* ssp.

Crimson fountain grass – *Pennisetum sectum* 'Rubrum'

Deer grass – *Muhlenbergia rigens*

Diamond grass – *Calamagrostis brachytricha*

Ethiopean fountain grass – *Pennisetum villosum*

Europian feather grass – *Stipa tenuissima*

Fairy grass – *Deschampsia flexuosa*

Feather grasses – *Stipa* ssp.

Feather reed grass – *Calamagrostix xacutaflora*

Fountain grass – *Pennisetum alopecuroides*

Foxtail grass – *Alopecurus pratensis*

Foxtail millet – *Setaria macrostachys*

Giant reed – *Arundo donax*

Golden Hakone grass – *Hakonechloa macra* 'Aureola'

Great weeping sedge – *Carex pendula*

Greater pond sedge – *Carex riparia*

Greater quaking grass – *Briza maxima*

Hair grass – *Deschampsia caespitose*

Hakone grass – *Hakonechloa macra*

Hardrush – *Juncus inflexus*

Hares tail – *Lagurus ovatus*

Indian grass – *Sorphastum nutans*

Japanese blood grass – *Imperata cylindrica* 'Rubra'

Job's tears – *Coix lacryma-jobi*

Large quaking grass – *Briza maxima*

Lesser quaking grass – *Briza media*

Lesser reedmace – *Typha minima*

Mosquito grass – *Bouteloua gracilis*

Needle grass – *Stipa* ssp.

Pampas grass – *Cortaderia selloana*

Panic grass – *Panicum virgatum*

Papyrus – *Cyperus papyrus*

Penduolous sedge – *Carex pendula*

Perennial quaking grass – *Briza media*

Pheasant tail grass – *Anementhele lessoniana*

Pony tail grass – *Stipa tenuissima*

Provencal reed – *Arundo donax*

Purple moor grass – *Molinia caerulea* ssp. *Caerulea*

Red New Zealand hook sedge – *Uncinia unciniata rubra*

Ribbon grass – *Phalaris arundinacea*

Sand love grass – *Eragrostis trichoides*

Smilo grass – *Oryzopsis miliaecea*

Snowy woodrush – *Luzula nivea*

Soft rush – *Juncus effusus*

Spanish oat grass – *Stipa gigantea*

Squirrel tail barley – *Hordum jubatum*

Switch grass – *Panicum virgatum*

Umbrella plants – *cyperus* ssp.

Weeping sedge – *Carex pendula*

Wood melic – *Melica uniflora*

Woodrush – *Luzula sylvatica*

Yorkshire fog – *Holcus lanatus*

Zebra grass – *Miscanthus sinensis* 'Zebrinus'

Bibliography

Buczacki, Stefan, and Harris, Keith, *Collins Guide to the Pests, Diseases and Disorders of Garden Plants* (Collins, 1981)

Costello, Lucinda, *Grasses and Bamboos* (Gmr, 2008)

Darke, Rick, *The Encyclopedia of Grasses for Livable Landscapes* (Timber Press, 2007)

Grounds, Roger, *Ornamental Grasses* (Christopher Helm, 1989)

King, Michael, and Oudolf, Piet, *Gardening with Grasses* (Frances Lincoln, 1998)

Lucas, Neil, *Designing with Grasses* (Timber Press, 2011)

Parkinson, Anna, *Nature's Alchemist: John Parkinson, herbalist to Charles I* (Frances Lincoln, 2007)

Robinson, William, *The Wild Garden* (The Collins Press, 2010)

Sudden, Andrew, *Longman Illustrated Dictionary of Botany* (Longman: York Press, 1984)

Wood, Trevor, *Garden Grasses, Rushes and Sedges* (John Wood)

Wulf, Andrea, *The Brother Gardeners: botany, empire and the birth of an obsession* (Windmill Books , 2009)

Useful addresses

WHERE TO SEE GRASSES

United Kingdom

Beth Chatto Gardens, Elmstead Market, Colchester, CO7 7DB
www.bethchatto.co.uk

Blooms of Bressingham, Bressingham, Diss, Norfolk, IP22 2PB
www.bloomsofbressingham.co.uk

Cambo House, Kingsbarn, St Andrews, Fife, KY16 8QD
www.camboestate.com

Knoll Gardens, Hampreston, Wimborne, Dorset, BH21 7ND
www.knollgardens.co.uk

Lady Farm Gardens, Lady Farm, Chelwood, Somerset, BS39 4NN
www.ladyfarm.com

Pensthorpe, Fakenham Road, Fakenham, Norfolk, NR21 0LN
www.pensthorpe.com

The Royal Botanic Gardens Kew, Richmond, Surrey, TW9 3AE
www.kew.org

The RHS Garden Harlow Carr, Crag Lane, Harrogate, North Yorkshire, HG3 1QB
www.rhs.org.uk

The RHS Garden Hyde Hall, Buckhatch Lane, Rettendon, Chelmsford, Essex, CM3 8ET
www.rhs.org.uk

The RHS Garden Rosemoor, Great Torrington, Devon, EX38 8PH
www.rhs.org.uk

The RHS Garden Wisley, Wisley, Woking, Surrey, GU23 6QB
www.rhs.org.uk

Scampston Hall, Malton, North Yorkshire, YO17 8NG
www.scampston.co.uk

Sir Harold Hillier Gardens, Jermyns Lane, Ampfield, Romsey, Hampshire, SO51 0QA
www.hilliergardens.org.uk

The Trentham Estate, Stone Road, Trentham, Stoke on Trent, ST4 8JG
www.trenthamleisure.co.uk

Europe

Berggarten Hannover, K+Herrenhausen Str 4, 30419 Hannover, Germany
www.berggarten-hannover.de

Karl-Foerster Garten, Am Raublang 6, 14469 Potsdam, Bornim, Germany

Hermannshof, Babostrasse 5, D-69469, Weinheim/ Bergstasse, Germany
www.sichtungsgarten-hermannshof.de

Le Jardin Plume, 76116 Auzouville sur Ry, France
www.lejardinplume.com

Lehrgaerten Weihenstephan, Am Staudengarten 9, 85350 Freising, Munich, Germany
www.hswt.de

Oudolf Nursery, Broekstraat 17, 6999 DE Hammelo, Netherlands.
www.oudolf.com

Overdam Nursery, Agiltevej 11, DK-2970 Horsholm, Denmark
www.overdam.dk

Priona Gardens, Schuinoslootweg 13, 7777RE, Schuinesloot, Netherlands
www.prionatuinen.com

Westpark, West Street, 80539, Munich, Germany

United States

The Battery Promenade and the Gardens of Remembrance, New York, New York
www.thebattery.org

Chanticleer Gardens, 786 Church Road, Wayne, Pennsylvania 19087
www.chanticleergarden.org

Chicago Botanic Gardens, 1000 Lake Cook Road, Glencoa, Illinois 60022
www.chicago-botanic.org

The High Line, New York, New York
www.thehighline.org

Huntington Botanical Gardens, 1151 Osford Road, San Marino, California 91108
www.huntington.org

Leaning Pine Arboretum, Calpoly State University, San Luis Obispo, California 93407
www.leaningpinearboretum.calpoly.edu

Longwood gardens, US Routel, PO Box 501, Kennett Square, Pennsylvania 19348
www.longwoodgardens.org

Lurie Gardens, Millenium Park, The Welcome Centre, 201 E Randolph Street, Chicago, Illinois
www.milleniumpark.org

Mt. Cuba Centre Inc, 3012 Barley Mill Road, Hockenssin, Delaware 19707
www.mtcubacenter.org

Native Sons. Inc., 379 W El Campo Road, Arroyo Grande, California 93420
www.nativeson.com

Rancho Santa Ana Botanic Garden, 1500 North College Avenue, Claremont, California 91711
www.rsabg.org

Regional Parks Botanic Garden, Wildcat Canyon Road, c/o Tilden Regional Park, Berkeley, California 94708-2396
www.nativeplants.org and www.ebparks.org

San Diego Zoo's Wild Animal Park, 15500 San Pasqual Valley Road, Escondido, California 92027 – 7017
www.sandiegozoo.org

San Francisco Botanical Garden at Strybing Arboretum, Ninth Avenue at Lincoln Way, San Francisco, California 94122
www.sfbotanicalgarden.org

The Santa Barbata Botanic Garden, 1212 Mission Canyon Road, Santa Barbara, California 93105
www.sbbg.org

The Scott Arboretum of Swarthmore College, 500 College Avenue, Swarthmore, Pennsylvania 19081
www.scottarboretum.org

Springs Preserve, 333 S Valley View Blud, between US95 and Alta Drive, Las Vegas, Nevada
www.springspreserve.org

WHERE TO BUY GRASSES

Happily today it is possible to buy grasses at most nurseries and garden centres. The following list is just a small selection of places that specialize in the sale of ornamental grasses. Omission from the list does in no way imply that other outlets are not of the same quality as those listed.

United Kingdom

The Alpine and Grass Nursery, Northgate, Pinchbeck, Spalding, Lincolnshire, PE11 3TB.
www.alpineandgrasses.co.uk

Beth Chatto Gardens, Elmstead Market, Colchester, Essex, CO7 7DB
www.bethchatto.co.uk

The Big Grass Company, Hookhill Plantation, Woolfardisworthy, East Devon, EX17 4RX
www.big-grass.com

Blooms of Bressingham, Bressingham, Diss, Norfolk, IP22 2AB
www.bloomsofbressingham.co.uk

Eversley Nursery, 10 Granville Avenue, Hesketh Bank, Preston, Lancashire, PR4 6AH
www.eversleynursery,co.uk

Foxgrove Plants, Skinners Green, Enborne, Newbury, Berkshire, RG14 6RE
www.foxgroveplants.co.uk

Hoecroft Plants, Severals Grange, Holt Road, Wood Norton, Dereham, Norfolk, NR20 5BL
www.hoecroft.co.uk

Knoll Gardens, Hampreston, Wimborne, Dorset, BH21 7ND
www.knollgardens.co.uk

Marchants Hardy Plants, 2 Marchants Cottages, Mill Lane, Laughton, East Sussex, BN8 6AJ
www.marchantshardyplants.co.uk

Oak Tree Nursery, Mill Lane, Barlow, Selby, North Yorkshire, YO8 8EY
www.oaktreenursery.com

The Plantsmans Preference, Hopton Road, Garboldisham, Diss, Norfolk, IP22 2QN
www.plantpref.co.uk

The RHS Garden Harlow Carr, Crag Lane, Harrogate, North Yorkshire, HG3 1QB
www.rhs.org.uk

The RHS Garden Hyde Hall, Backhatch Lane, Rettendon, Chelmsford, Essex, CM3 8ET
www.rhs.org.uk

The RHS Garden Rosemoor, Great Torrington, Devon, EX38 8PH
www.rhs.org.uk

The RHS Garden Wisley, Wisley, Woking, Surrey, GU23 6QB
www.rhs.org.uk

Scampston Hall, Malton, North Yorkshire, YO17 8NG
www.scampston.co.uk

NURSERIES GROWING RESTIOS

Churchtown Nursery, Little Kenegic, Gulval, Penzance, Cornwall, TR20 8YN
www.kelnanplants.com

Trewidden Nursery, Buryas Bridge, Penzance, Cornwall, TR20 8TT
www.trewidden-online.co.uk

Europe

Bamboos de Planbuisson, Rue Montaigne, 24480, Le Buisson de Cadouin, France
www.planbuisson.com

Le Jardin Plume, 76116 Auzouville sur Ry, France
www.lejardinplume.com

Oudolf Nursery, Broekstraat 17, 6999 De Hummelo, Netherlands
www.oudolf.com

Overdam Nursery, Agiltevej 11, DK-2970,, Horsholm, Denmark
www.overdam.dk

Staudengaertner Klose, Rosenstrasse 10, D-34253, Lohfeldon, Germany
www.staudengaertner-klose.de

USA

Berkeley Horticultural Nursery, 1310 McGee Avenue, Berkeley, California 94703
www.berkeleyhort.com

Daryll's Nursery, 15770 Ellendale Road, Dallas, Oregon 97338
www.daryllsnursery.com

Digging Dog Nursery, PO Box 471, Albion, California 95410
www.diggingdog.com

Earthly Pursuits Inc., 290 Kuntz Road, Windsor Mill, Maryland 21244
www.earthlypursuits.net

Greenlee Nursery Inc, 6075, Kimball Avenue, Chino, California, 91780
www.greenleenursery.com

High Country Gardens, 2902 Rutina Street, Santa Fe, New Mexico 87507
www.highcountrygardens.com

Hoffman Nursery, 5520 Bahama Road, Rougemont, North Carolina 27572
www.hoffmannursery.com

Kurt Bluemel Inc, 2740 Greene Lane, Baldwin, Maryland 21013
www.kurtbluemel.com

Mostly Native Nursery, PO Box 258, 27235 Highway One, Tomales, California 94971
www.mostlynatives.com

Mountain States Wholesale Nursery, PO Box 2500, Litchfield Park, Arizona 85340
www.mswn.com

The Native Plant Nursery, PO Box 7841, Ann Arbor, Michigan 48107
www.nativeplant.com

Native Sons Wholesale, 379 W, El Campo Road, Arryo Grande, California 93420
www.nativeson.com

North Creek Nurseries Wholesale, RR2, Box 33, Landenberg, Pennsylvania 19350
www.northcreeknurseries.com

Northwind Perennial Farm, 7047 Hospital Road, Burlington, Wisconsin 53105
www.northwindperennialfarm.com

Pinelands Nursery, 323 Island Road, Columbus, New Jersey 09022
www.pinelandsnursery.com

Plant Delights Nursery, 9241 Sauls Road, Raleigh, North Carolina 27603
www.plantdelights.com

Plants of the Southwest, Agna Fria, Route 6, Box 11A, Santa Fe, New Mexico 87501
www.plantsofthesouthwest.com

Steve Schmidt Nursery, PO Box 53, 29977, S E Weitz Lane, Eagle Creek, Oregon 97022
www.steveschmidnursery.com

Triple Oaks Nursery, PO Box 385, 2359 S Delsea Drive, Franklinville, New Jersey 08322
www.tripleoaks.com

Walla Walla Nursery Co, 4176 Stateline Road, Walla Walla, Washington 99362
www.wallawallanursery.com

Wildtype Design, Native Plants and Seeds, 900 N Every Road, Mason, Michigan 28854
www.wildtypeplants.com

Wind Poppy Farm and Nursery, 3171 Unick Road, Ferndale, Washington 98248
www.windpoppy.com

Canada

Bluestem Nursery, 16 Kingsley Road, Christina Lake, British Columbia, VOH 1E3
www.bluestem.ca

WHERE TO BUY SEED

Many of the previously listed nurseries will sell seed as well as plants. The following is a list of purely seed merchants.

United Kingdom

Chilterns Seeds, Bortree Stile, Ulverston, Cumbria, LA12 7PB
www.chilternsseeds.co.uk

Jellito Perennial Seeds, PO Box 78, St Ives, Huntingdon, Cambridgeshire, PE27 6ZB
www.jelitto.com

Moles Seeds (UK) Ltd, Turkey Cock Lane, Stanway, Colchester, Essex, CO3 8PD
www.molesseeds.co.uk

Plant World Seeds, St Marychurch Road, Newton Abbot, Devon, TQ12 4SE
www.plant-world-seeds.com

United States

Granite Seed, 1697 W.2100 North Lehi, Utah 84043
www.graniteseed.com

Jellito Perennial Seeds, 125 Chenoweth Lane, Suite 301, Louisville, Kentucky 40207
www.jellito.com

Larner Seeds, PO Box 407, Bolinas, California 94924
www.larnerseeds.com

Stock Seed Farm, 28008 Mill Road, Murdock, Nebraska 68407
www.stockseed.com

Western Native Seed, PO Box 188, Coaldale, Colorado 81222
www.westernnativeseed.com

Wind River Seeds, 3075 Lane 51(half), Manderson, Wyoming 82432
www.windriverseed.com

Index

Numbers in **bold** indicate a picture.